Offa

Volume 1 for 2019

Aims and Scope

Offa's Dyke Journal is a venue for the publication of high-quality research on the archaeology, history and heritage of frontiers and borderlands focusing on the Anglo-Welsh border. The editors invite submissions that explore dimensions of Offa's Dyke, Wat's Dyke and the 'short dykes' of western Britain, including their life-histories and landscape contexts. *ODJ* will also consider comparative studies on the material culture and monumentality of frontiers and borderlands from elsewhere in Britain, Europe and beyond. We accept:

1. Notes of up to 3,000 words

2. Interim reports on fieldwork of up to 5,000 words

3. Original discussions, syntheses and analyses of up to 10,000 words

ODJ is published by JAS Arqueología, and is supported by the University of Chester and the Offa's Dyke Association. The journal is open access, free to authors and readers: http://revistas.jasarqueologia.es/index.php/odjournal/.

Print copies of the journal are available for purchase from Archaeopress with a discount available for members of the Offa's Dyke Association: https://www.archaeopress.com/

Editors

Professor Howard Williams BSc MA PhD FSA (Professor of Archaeology, University of Chester)
Email: howard.williams@chester.ac.uk

Liam Delaney BA MA MCIfA (Doctoral Researcher, University of Chester)
Email: 1816919@chester.ac.uk.

Submissions: odj@chester.ac.uk

Front cover: Drone photograph of Offa's Dyke on Llanfair Hill, looking north (Photograph: Julian Ravest). Cover and logo design by Howard Williams and Liam Delaney, with thanks to Tim Grady and Adam Parsons for critical input.

This printed edition published by Archaeopress in association with JAS Arqueología, and supported by the University of Chester and the Offa's Dyke Association.

ISBN 978-1-78969-538-0

ISSN of the online edition 2695-625X

Offa's Dyke Journal

Volume 1 for 2019

Edited by Howard Williams and Liam Delaney

University of Chester

Offa's Dyke Journal

Volume 1 for 2019

The Offa's Dyke Collaboratory
and the Offa's Dyke Journal

Howard Williams and Liam Delaney

Opening the first volume of a new open-access peer-reviewed academic publication, we are pleased to introduce the Offa's Dyke Journal. This venture stems from the activities of the Offa's Dyke Collaboratory, a research network founded in April 2017 to foster and support new research on the monuments and landscapes of the Anglo-Welsh borderlands and comparative studies of borderlands and frontiers from prehistory to the present. The proceedings of a series of academic and public-facing events have informed the character and direction of the Journal. Moreover, its establishment coincides with the Cadw/Historic England/Offa's Dyke Association-funded Offa's Dyke Conservation Management Plan as well as other new community and research projects on linear earthworks. Funded by the University of Chester and the Offa's Dyke Association, and published online by JAS Arqueologia and print-distributed by Archaeopress, the journal aims to provide a resource for scholars, students and the wider public regarding the archaeology, heritage and history of the Welsh Marches and its linear monuments. It also delivers a much-needed venue for interdisciplinary studies from other times and places.

Keywords: borders, borderlands, dykes, frontiers, linear earthworks, walls

> Offa's Dyke does not explain itself to you. Whilst it is a superb walk, one learns surprisingly little from traversing its length. In fact, it is noticeable that the many visitors who are walking the long-distance footpath quickly accept the Dyke and become fixated on the number of miles they have covered. The Dyke has not inspired a Rudyard Kipling, who wrote of the garrison on Hadrian's Wall, nor do we have a mental image of the Saxons to put beside the Hollywood image of Rome, nor an understanding of the people of the kingdom of the Mercians over whom Offa ruled. (Hill and Worthington 2003: 9)

Introduction

For this first-ever volume of the *Offa's Dyke Journal*, we offer a three-part Introduction. First, we review recent work on linear monuments as frontiers and borderlands. Next, we survey the development and activities of the Offa's Dyke Collaboratory to date. Finally, we introduce the *Offa's Dyke Journal* itself and the contents of Volume 1.

From the Devil's Dyke of Cambridgeshire to the Danevirke, from the Elbe to the Danube, early medieval frontiers and borderlands remain poorly researched. For example, Britain's

Offa's Dyke Journal volume 1 2019
Manuscript received: 29 November 2019
accepted: 6 December 2019

Figure 1: Offa's Dyke at Dudston Fields, Montgomeyshire, looking south. This is a well-preserved section of the monument with the bank and ditch surviving on a significant scale, but ongoing erosion caused by livestock is evident in the foreground (Photograph: Howard Williams, 2019)

Figure 2: East Wansdyke on Morgan's Hill, Wiltshire, looking east. (Photograph: Howard Williams, 2016)

Figure 3: Aerial photograph of the undated Row Ditch (Herefordshire) looking north-north-west. The continuous nature of the monument is evident; it survives in field boundaries but its near-obliteration in the foreground leaves only a subtle trace of its former route. (Musson, C.R. 03-C-1254. Herefordshire Archaeological Survey 2003: 31/08/2003)

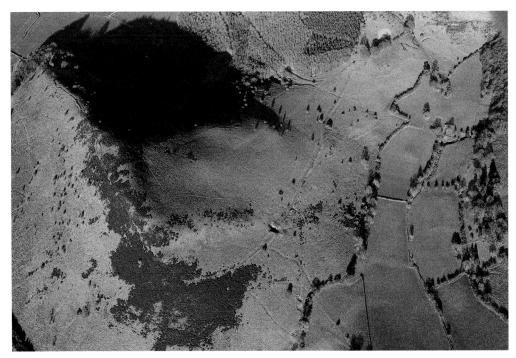

Figure 4: Aerial photograph of Herrock and Rushock Hills (Powys) orientated c. north-east. Offa's Dyke ascends (top-left) and wraps around the summit of Herrock Hill before running up to Rushock Hill (top-right). (Musson, C. R. 06-CN-1009. Herefordshire Aerial Archaeological Survey 2006: 04/05/2006)

longest linear earthwork, Offa's Dyke, has only received detailed modern survey in one well-preserved location (Everson 1991; Ray and Bapty 2016: 194–98; Figure 1). Linear earthworks are difficult to survey and map. Their impressive scale – running often for many kilometres – can make them notable landscape features, as with East Wansdyke in Wiltshire (Fox and Fox 1958; Reynolds and Langlands 2006) (Figure 2). Yet equally, their vast extent and monumentality can be a challenge to securely discerning the scale and character as they run over different geologies, topographies, and through different subsequent land uses. Whilst their banks, ditches and associated earthwork features are often expected to endure for centuries, they can be rapidly erased in only a relative short time, especially in the modern era (e.g. Belford 2017). The Rowe Ditch in Herefordshire illustrates this point: it survives preserved in field boundaries over a long distance, only to be replaced by a heavily denuded earthwork where it no longer is marked by a hedge (Figure 3). Likewise, Offa's Dyke can be charted on the ground and from the air as it dramatically wraps around Herrock Hill and continues eastwards to Rushock Hill (Powys) (Figure 4), yet the monument is lost where it crosses the river valley of the Riddings and Hindwell brooks to the north and it likewise has been lost where it drops off Rushock Hill to the east. Indeed, the continuance of the Dyke eastwards from this point is a topic of ongoing academic debate (Hill and Worthington 2003: 50, 129–33; Bapty 2004; Ray and Bapty 2016: 46, 49, 128).

Whether called 'earthworks', 'walls', 'ramparts' or 'dykes', linear monuments may remain 'lost' or uncertain over long distances, suspected only by references in place-names, old maps, or preserved in the lines of later features. Many short dykes survive in a fragmentary state, are elusive to the observer, and many remain undated (Malim *et al.* 1997; Hankinson and Caseldine 2006; Worthington Hill and Grigg 2015; Grigg 2018).

These are some of the reasons why linear monuments can often languish undated and only partially defined. Consequently, many have floated outside of historical and archaeological narratives as enigmas in the landscape, or else tied to narratives of warfare and territoriality without solid and detailed evidence for their date, design or disposition. Hence, as Hill and Worthington (2003: 9) note in the above quotation, even dedicated and knowledgeable visitors as well as those living in their proximity for decades often struggle to apprehend and appreciate where they are and what they are. Furthermore, dykes are often situated within and beyond individual locales, defying clear and simple senses of affinity and place-making by local people and visitors, and frustrating recognition by those attempting to chart their course. Despite a long history of antiquarian and archaeological investigations, enquiry and speculation since before the birth of the modern disciplines of history and archaeology, linear earthworks remain a fascination yet inherently ambiguous and mutable among the public and scholars alike Rahtz 1961; Hill and Worthington 2003; Erskine 2007; Lennon 2010; Bell 2012; Tyler 2011; Ray and Bapty 2016). Indeed, studies dedicated to linear monuments remain relatively scarce. Again, Offa's Dyke is a case in point; in a century it has had numerous individual book chapters and journal articles, but only four book-length studies exist (Fox 1955; Noble 1983; Hill and Worthington 2003; Ray and Bapty 2016). Meanwhile, Britain's second-longest early medieval monument, Wat's Dyke, has received even more sparse treatment (Fox 1934; Worthington 1997; Malim and Hayes 2008; see also Hill 1974; 1991; 2000; 2001).

Yet there remains considerable potential for charting the lines of dykes, revealing their shifting monumentalities and significances via multiple lines of cross-disciplinary enquiry (e.g. Hardt 2005; Reynolds and Langlands 2006). Broader questions regarding how these monuments operated as parts of early medieval frontiers and borderlands, and how they were managed, evolved, abandoned, and repurposed remain to be explored, as ably demonstrated in recent work on Offa's Dyke (Ray and Bapty 2016; Belford 2017, this volume). Linear earthworks would have no doubt used parts of topographically defined and transformed frontiers which would have included other forms of natural marker, coasts, rivers and wetlands, heaths, woods and hills (Squatriti 2004). Not all early medieval frontiers and borderlands would have required linear earthworks to demarcate them, or even monuments of other kinds deployed in relation to a host of adapted natural features (Hardt 2005; Pohl 2005). Broader still, we need to appreciate early medieval frontiers and borderlands as more than lines or swathes in the landscape, but as zones of both mobility and control, which would have included settlements and fortifications, land and water routes (Brookes 2013; Baker and Brookes 2015). The potential for intensive and extensive archaeological investigations of linear monuments and their landscape context was reiterated and extended most recently by Ray and Bapty (2016), and the results of such work are evident in the rich results of fieldwor: both surveys (e.g. Everson 1991) and excavations (e.g. Allen 1988; Malim *et al.* 1997; Hankinson and Caseldine 2006; Malim 2007; Malim and Hayes 2008; Belford 2017; Ladd and Mortimer 2017). Place-name evidence can be incredibly revealing (e.g. Gelling 1992; Hardt 2005) and landscape contexts for monuments require further detailed attention, taking into account those affected by, and in opposition to, frontiers as much as a focus on their creators (e.g. Edwards 2009; Murrieta-Flores and Williams 2017). The study of these linear monuments therefore requires us to investigate their construction and placement, broader multi-scalar landscape contexts and their biographies of use and reuse (Belford 2017; Ray and Bapty 2016; Murrieta-Flores and Williams 2017).

Interpretive barriers to understanding early medieval frontier works are often as significant as practical and methodological challenges. For instance, there remains a tendency to consider dykes as hard borders and military barriers rather than permeable, fluid and transformative zones of social, economic, political and cultural interaction. Whether they are constituted as enduring formulations with lasting legacies through into the modern world or elements of seemingly fleeting and fluctuating arrangements, we increasingly understand the challenges of imposing modern ideas of borders, as well as presuming contemporaneous or later literary conceptions reflect past realities (Curta 2005: 2–3). Rather than stark dividing lines between peoples and kingdoms, between 'barbarians' and 'civilization', they are more profitably considered as complex borderland zones and frontier networks. Some regard early medieval linear works as related to frontiers, but primarily as defensive military features, and indeed there are many profitable directions for considering their military uses and contexts (Grigg 2014; 2018; Reynolds 2013). Yet many entertain their potential socio-economic, political and ideological roles, and more complex relationships: monuments used to create and transform borderlands into frontiers, and monuments with multiple roles and significances (Ray and Bapty 2016: 334–64; see also Squatriti 2002; 2004; Wileman 2003). Considering how dykes were built and used to control and manage, facilitate and foster, interactions and communications as well as the movements of people, animals and resources helps us to put these monuments into the landscape and back into history (Brookes 2013). Moreover, frontier zones and their built dimensions were elements of sophisticated and shifting practices of spatial manipulation and territoriality invested with ideological and symbolic associations (Squatriti 2002; 2004; 2006; Curta 2005; Pohl 2005: 261–262; ; see also Hingley 2012; Maldonado 2015). This formulation of ethnic and social groupings might be seen as helped, as well as hindered, by the formulation and perpetuation of frontier zones from Late Antiquity to the later Middle Ages (e.g. Brather 2005). Adapting and reconfiguring Roman ideas and material traces, early medieval frontiers were complex and varied in scale and form, use and enduring significances. Furthermore, as physical traces of past times, earthworks and other monuments in frontier zones might foster and perpetuate all manner of fantastical, legendary and

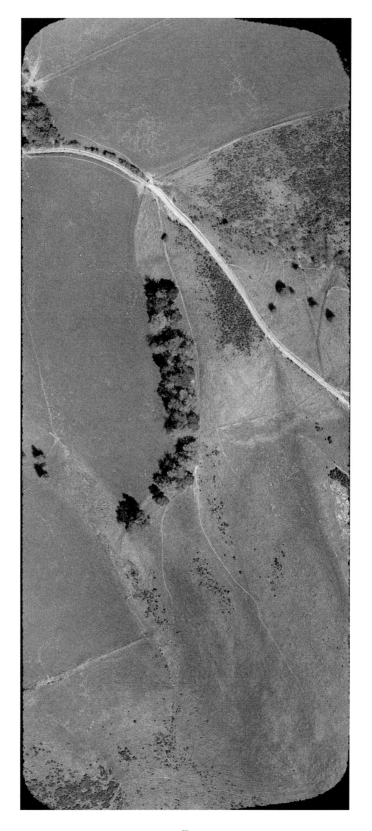

Figure 5: Drone photograph of Cwmsanahan Hill (Shropshire) where Offa's Dyke ascends and incorporates a summit, adapting to the steep topography by taking a series of stepped angled turns. N to top of the image. (Photograph: Julian Ravest)

historically grounded stories for early medieval communities and kingdoms (Pohl 2005: 257; Wileman 2003). Notwithstanding, the after-lives of these monuments are as intriguing as their construction and use, sometimes setting up traditions of frontier organisation of a very different nature and context both in the Anglo-Welsh borderlands and elsewhere (Swallow 2016; see also Bartlett and MacKay 1989), in other instances becoming powerful and evocative in myth and legend, mobilised in varied social and ideological contexts through their incongruity and redundancy.

Researchers are beginning to tackle these questions afresh, armed with a wider set of comparative perspectives. In recent decades there has been a clear growth in research on frontiers and borderlands across disciplines and time periods. These include well-established and varied research foci: prehistoric territorial divisions (DeAtley and Findlow 1984; Lewis 2012: 49–57); time-depth of frontier works (Bowen 1990: 15–41); frontiers of ancient empires, especially of Roman frontiers (Hingley 2008, 2012; Breeze 2018); and the afterlives of frontiers (Collins 2012; Hingley 2012; Maldonado 2015); the emergence of medieval frontiers (Dobat 2008), but also investigating the frontiers of modern nation-states and the complex issues with contemporary borders (Konrad and Brunet-Jailly 2019), mobility in relation to those (see Fryde and Reitz 2009; Mullin 2011a and b; Hamilakis 2018) and identity (Flynn 2008: 311–330). These include rich and varied approaches to the study of borders, borderlands and frontiers in the contemporary world in both material and metaphorical terms (e.g. McAtackney 2015; McWilliams 2013). Due to the nature of borderlands and frontiers, this topic can also cover discussions around imperialism and nationalism. Hence, our work should not shy away from evaluating the contentious topics of the construction and maintenance of borders to restrict freedom of movement (Boozer 2018: 206–39, Fauser et al. 2019: 483–88) From a research perspective this topic is energised in many different disciplines, debating issues around linear earthworks which includes why frontiers were created, how they functioned and the occurrence of their demise.

This growth in research interest has been bolstered by advancements in field survey including improvements and large-scale acceptance of new digital heritage technology and survey techniques of data collection, resolution, access, processing and visualisation (Bennett et al. 2013: 197–206). In addition to the long-term use of a host of survey methods, including aerial photography and satellite images to chart their courses (e.g. Alibaigi 2019; see Figures 4 and 5), now it is possible for large landscape monuments, such as linear monuments (including dykes) to take on a whole new life when they are visualised digitally. Due to their size, these monuments are incredibly difficult to comprehend on the ground, and this is further complicated when in woodland or

Figure 6 (next page): Re-Mapping Offa's Dyke on Garnon's Hill: (a) Garnon's Hill with dashed line indicating previously projected route of dyke and solid line indicating new route of dyke after investigation. SVF DTM created from 2m lidar model; (b) Offa's Dyke on Garnon's Hill, having just crested the ridge, facing south; (c) Offa's Dyke on Garnon's Hill, ascending the hill, facing south-east; (d) 3D Relief Model in planlaufterrain, Offa's Dyke is highlighted

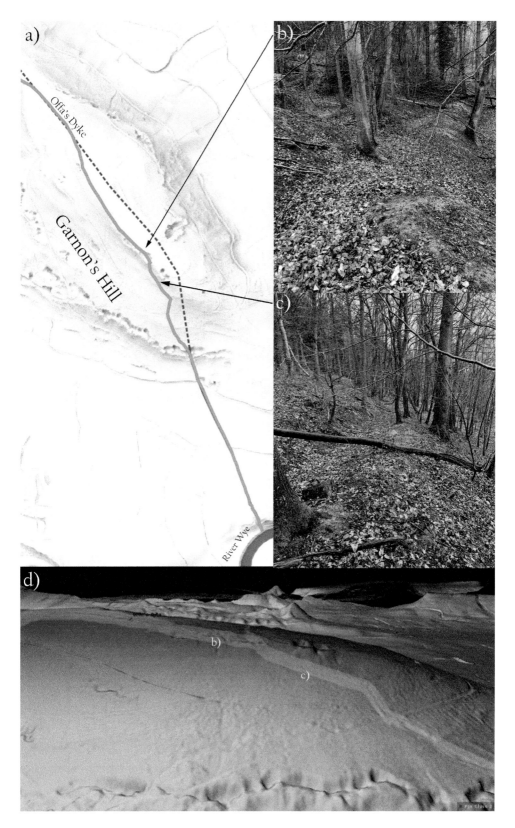

equally impassable or visually restrictive environments, which hampers traditional survey greatly. Utilising digital models means these earthworks and landscapes can be explored, measured and visualised in a way that would have been impossible prior to the advent of these tools. This dataset is boosted by the accessibility of unmanned aerial vehicles (UAVs), or drones, which are able to, very rapidly, capture images of these features from low altitudes. This results in stunning and informative images and models allows us the ability to see and study in a way which is impossible to do on the ground and before would have required expensive chartered flights (see: the work of Julian Ravest (2019); Figure 5). Lidar, especially, facilitates the quick creation of accurate digital terrain models that have been stripped of vegetation and land-cover, allowing an unobstructed view not only the earthworks but of minor topographical and surface expressions. This is especially useful when looking at large linear earthworks, whose route may be obscured by thick woodland, or potentially have been ploughed out and destroyed in later periods. The utilisation of digital survey methods is allowing discovery and precise mapping of archaeological landscapes like National Parks (Hesse 2013: 171–83, New Forest National Park 2018,), large landscape monuments like hillforts (Murray 2018) and linear earthworks such as the Antonine Wall (Hannon 2018) or the Black Pigs Dyke (O' Drisceoil et al. 2014: 32–34) for possibly the first time.

This approach to linear earthworks is no better exemplified by the ongoing doctoral research by one of us (Liam Delaney) on Offa's Dyke, looking at the route through Herefordshire. Garnon's Hill, on the north banks of the River Wye, is classically recorded as the last hilltop that Offa's Dyke navigates before it descends, and crosses the plains until hitting the north banks of the Wye. It is not to be seen again until north Gloucestershire (Fox 1955: 181). Garnon's Hill is in an area of incredible dense woodland which makes terrestrial survey especially difficult here. This has possibly contributed to why it has been questioned whether it have was present across the Herefordshire plain. Notably, during the Offa's Dyke Project, David Hill and Margaret Worthington Hill undertook exploratory excavation here in the 1970s but could not find any sign of the earthwork and subsequently ruled out of the existence of the dyke here (Hill and Worthington 2003: 137–39). However, their excavation location was based upon early mapping of the route of the dyke which imagined the monument had run along the ridge of the hill – an unusual behaviour for the dyke because elsewhere it can be shown to have repeatedly navigated the western sides and shoulders of hills. To investigate the Dyke on Garnon's Hill a digital terrain model was created from lidar data. The model showed an earthwork which was continuous from the north banks of the Wye. It can be seen ascending the hill on the south side before taking a sharp right-angled turn and skirting the ridge, before descending again on the north side (Figure 6). These are all behaviours of the dyke which are regular on other lengths and hills. GPS points were taken off the digital model, which facilitated a ground-truthing survey to confirm the digital mapping predictions. This meant that Offa's Dyke was accurately mapped and confirmed on this hill for the first time. Repeating this methodology is producing results along the route of the dyke and is opening up new research possibilities for the study of large linear earthworks elsewhere.

Figure 7: The Offa's Dyke Collaboratory bilingual logo designed by former University of Chester student Jonathan Felgate

Figure 8: Presenters at the Offa's Dyke Collaboratory Inaugural Workshop organised by Howard Williams, Patricia Murrieta-Flores and James Pardoe, University Centre Shrewsbury, 28 April 2017: Tim Malim (top-left), Stuart Brookes (top-right), David Parsons (bottom-left) and Rachel Swallow (bottom-right). For details see: https://offaswatsdyke.wordpress.com/odc-events/offas-dyke-collaboratory-the-university-centre-shrewsbury-inaugural-workshop/

Figure 9: Delegates attending the Offa's Dyke Collaboratory Inaugural Workshop, 28 April 2017 (left-to-right: Rachel Swallow, Bob Silvester, David McGlade, Peter Reavill, Tim Malim, Andy Seaman, Jeremy Haslam, Bill Klemperer, Charles Insley, Mark Redknap, Keith Ray, David Persons, Christopher Catling, John Hunt, Roger White, Louise Barker, Rhiannon Comeau, John Baker, Will Davies, Tim Hoverd, Alison MacDonald, Ian Dormer, Rob Dingle, Alice Thorne, Morn Capper, Hugh Hannaford, Giles Carey, Gary Duckers, Patricia Murrieta-Flores, Andrew Blake, Brian Costello, Jessica Murray, Kate Biggs, Stuart Brookes, Alessandra Perrone, Mel Barge, Margaret Worthington Hill, Alex Langlands, Sue Evans, John Hoyle, Andy Wigley, Paul Belford, Caroline Pudney, Seren Griffiths, Howard Williams); inset: the afternoon 'round table' discussion at the Offa's Dyke Collaboratory Inaugural Workshop

The public remain at the heart of many studies of linear earthworks, although there is debate about how public archaeology and heritage can potentially contribute to the study of linear earthworks and their borderland context. For instance, many people and communities have engaged directly with the archaeology of Offa's Dyke and Wat's Dyke over the years, including the production of its archaeological narrative. Notably, volunteers worked with David Hill and Margaret Worthington Hill on their projects over thirty years (Hill and Worthington 2003: 8). More recently, projects with the Clwyd-Powys Archaeological Trust and partners and the Wye Valley Area of Outstanding Natural Beauty illustrate the continuation of this legacy for the study, promotion and conservation of both monuments. There are also those who have no immediate interest in the archaeology but nevertheless appreciate the many layers of landscape history which are revealed when walking the trails along both dykes. For many members of the Offa's Dyke Association, for example, the earthworks themselves are just one part of a much broader experience that includes ecology, biodiversity, and physical and mental wellbeing. There are therefore many wider issues in public engagement, from working with specific vulnerable groups to engaging with communities to foster their sense of ownership, place, history and identity.

The Offa's Dyke Collaboratory

Following a series of meetings during 2015 and 2016, the Offa's Dyke Collaboratory was established. The formation of the Collaboratory was born from discussions between its

Figure 10: Andy Seaman (left) and Melanie Roxby-Mackay (right) presenting at the Dykes through Time: Rethinking Early Medieval Linear Earthworks session at the 39th annual Theoretical Archaeology Group conference, Cardiff University, 18–20 December 2017

convenors,[1] who between them bring a range of expertise in archaeology and heritage from across the Anglo-Welsh borderlands and who represent a range of organisations, to build momentum for new research into Offa's Dyke, Wat's Dyke and their landscape contexts. These discussions took place in the light of the soon-to-be published monograph by Keith Ray and Ian Bapty (2016). Following the book's release, the convenors set about establishing workshops and conference sessions to develop dialogues across Wales, England and beyond to investigate Britain's largest and longest ancient monuments and, more broadly, the landscapes, monuments and material cultures of other frontiers and borderlands. Membership to the Collaboratory is free and open to anyone actively researching frontiers and borderlands; currently a host of organisations and a significant number of individual members have joined this network.[2] Its name is intended not to focus exclusively or even primarily on the components of linear earthworks traditionally dubbed 'Offa's Dyke'. Instead, Offa's Dyke is considered as a fulcrum around which broader research into archaeological, heritage and historical questions regarding linear monuments can pivot. This is also reflected in the use of the cross-section of the Dyke's bank and ditch in the design of the Collaboratory's logo, designed by former University of Chester student, Jonathan Felgate (Figure 7).

The Collaboratory exists through its Wordpress website and blog, which contains static pages about the Collaboratory, including links, resources, details of members and convenors, as well as links to the *Journal* and activities and notes on research questions, projects and agenda. In addition, it provides a platform for regular blog-posts on themes relating to the activities and work of the convenors and members: at the time of writing there have been 91

---

[1]   https://offaswatsdyke.wordpress.com/convenors/
[2]   https://offaswatsdyke.wordpress.com/odc-members/

Figure 11: Presenters at the Offa's Dyke Heritage work-shop organised by Howard Williams at the Offa's Dyke Centre, Knighton (Powys), 23 March 2018

posts.[3] Facebook[4] and Twitter[5] pages also help disseminate the Wordpress site's posts.

Collaboratory events

The events of the Collaboratory have directly informed the *Journal*'s content and character, and therefore they deserve a brief review in this first volume in order to provide context for this publication. The Collaboratory has already instigated a series of public-facing events and academic workshops/conferences. The first of these was the inaugural event held at University Centre Shrewsbury on 28 April 2017, organised by Howard Williams with Patricia Murrieta-Flores and James Pardoe.[6] This involved a morning of research papers outlining the latest thinking and discoveries on linear earthworks and their landscape contexts (Figure 8), and an afternoon round table chaired by archaeologist Caroline Pudney (University of Chester), featuring an important contribution by veteran investigator of Offa's Dyke and Wat's Dyke, Margaret Worthington Hill, and closing remarks by early medieval archaeologist and landscape researcher Andy Seaman. Over 70 individuals attended from a range of local societies, governmental bodies and heritage organisations from both Wales and England (Figure 9).[7]

This opening event set the precedent for a series of subsequent workshops and conferences, each with a different venue and focus. A second event took place as an

---

[3] https://offaswatsdyke.wordpress.com/
[4] https://www.facebook.com/OffasDykeCollaboratory/
[5] https://twitter.com/ODCollaboratory
[6] https://offaswatsdyke.wordpress.com/odc-events/offas-dyke-collaboratory-the-university-centre-shrewsbury-inaugural-workshop/
[7] https://offaswatsdyke.wordpress.com/odc-events/offas-dyke-collaboratory-the-university-centre-shrewsbury-inaugural-workshop/

Figure 12: Presenters at the Offa's Dyke Conference organised by CPAT on behalf of the Offa's Dyke Collaboratory, Marches School, Oswestry, 15 September 2018: Paul Belford, Keith Ray, Ray Bailey, Melanie Roxby-Mackay, and Dick Finch

academic conference session at the 39th annual Theoretical Archaeology Group meeting, held 18–20 December 2017 at Cardiff University. Entitled 'Dykes through Time: Rethinking Early Medieval Linear Earthworks'. The session was organised by Howard Williams with papers tackling the biographies and landscape contexts of linear monuments and their public perception today (Figure 10; see also Seaman this volume).[8]

---

[8] https://offaswatsdyke.wordpress.com/odc-events/dykes-through-time-rethinking-early-medieval-linear-earthworks-cardiff-tag-18-20-december-2017/

Figure 13: Visiting the CPAT excavations near Chirk Castle. Above: five of the six co-convenors of the Offa's Dyke Collaboratory: (left-to-right) Keith Ray, Howard Williams, David McGlade, Paul Belford and Andrew Blake. Below: Ian Grant of CPAT presents the results of the findings from the excavations (see Belford this volume)

The third event was again organised by Howard Williams and shifted the focus to heritage dimensions. The day-workshop hosted by the Offa's Dyke Centre at Knighton, Powys on 23 March 2018 was entitled 'Offa's Dyke Heritage'.[9] Papers and discussions here explored new strategies for management, conservation and interpretation of Offa's Dyke and Wat's Dyke, as well as considering the contemporary uses of linear monuments as landscapes of death and memory (Figure 11; see also Swogger this volume).

Having organised an inaugural gathering for specialists, an academic conference session and a heritage workshop, the next event was aimed to be a public-facing day conference, simply called 'The Offa's Dyke Conference'. Taking place 15 September 2018 at the Marches School, Oswestry and organised by Clwyd-Powys Archaeological Trust, the event brought together experts, local societies and enthusiasts with a focus on community archaeology and heritage activities taking place up and down the length of the Anglo-Welsh borderlands (Figure 12).[10] Presentations considered work in the Wye Valley, around Trefonen, Wrexham and Flintshire, followed by an afternoon trip to see the CPAT excavations at Chirk Castle (Figure 13; see also Belford this volume). They then visited the CPAT excavation of Offa's Dyke in the Chirk Castle estate.

The fifth principal Collaboratory event was a public day conference at the Grosvenor Museum, Chester, organised by University of Chester final-year archaeology students and

---

[9] https://offaswatsdyke.wordpress.com/odc-events/offas-dyke-heritage-23rd-march-2018/
[10] https://offaswatsdyke.wordpress.com/odc-events/the-offas-dyke-conference-oswestry-15th-september-2018/

Figure 14: Organised by CPAT at the Offa's Dyke Centre: The Offa's Dyke Living History Weekend, 13 July 2019. Advertisement for the event plus presentations by Niall Heaton (above) and Liam Delaney (below)

facilitated by Howard Williams on the theme of The Public Archaeology of Frontiers and Borderlands, 20 March 2019. As well as student presentations, there were special guest talks by Penelope Foreman, Keith Ray and John G. Swogger.[11] Together, these events have served to provide a basis for fresh perspectives and new research on the Anglo-Welsh borderland in comparative perspective and taking archaeological, heritage and interdisciplinary viewpoints.

It is important to recognise that these Collaboratory-organised events have been matched by a wide range of public-facing and academic activities and talks at which convenors have presented their research from 2017 to the present. Most recently these have included the CBA conference 'New Work on the Dyke', 30 March 2019,[12] and the Offa's Dyke AGM 50th Anniversary Weekend,[13] and CPAT's Living History Weekend,

[11]   https://offaswatsdyke.wordpress.com/odc-events/1473-2/
[12]   https://offaswatsdyke.wordpress.com/2019/04/04/the-cba-wales-conference-new-perspectives-on-the-dyke-30th-march-2019-offas-dyke-centre-knighton/
[13]   https://offaswatsdyke.wordpress.com/2019/04/29/offas-dyke-association-50th-anniversary-agm-weekend/

Figure 15: The Offa's Dyke Association 50th Anniversary Exhibition and Heritage Walk at Trefonen, Shropshire, with displays of the new marker posts to be raised at either end of the village on the Offa's Dyke Path (left) and display about Offa's Dyke by the local primary school

13–14 July 2019,[14] each taking place at the Offa's Dyke Centre, Knighton (Figure 14). Each co-convenor has been busy promoting and conducting research in different capacities. For example, one of us (Howard Williams) opened the Offa's Dyke Association 50th Anniversary Exhibition and Heritage Walk at Trefonen, Shropshire.[15] As well as exhibitions on local heritage, history, crafts and nature conservation, there was a display of Offa's Dyke by the local primary school, and the unveiling of two new heritage posts to mark the Offa's Dyke Path at either end of the village (Figure 15). Furthermore, future Collaboratory events have been proposed and planned, with possible sessions taking place at international academic conferences as well as public-facing events during 2020: details will be announced via the Collaboratory website.

The Collaboratory in context

We recognise that the Collaboratory has developed alongside other endeavours currently underway relating to linear monuments of the Anglo-Welsh borderlands. The Offa's Dyke Conservation Management Plan (CMP), for example, was initiated alongside the Collaboratory by a triumvirate of agencies (Cadw, Historic England and the Offa's Dyke

---

[14] https://offaswatsdyke.wordpress.com/2019/05/31/knighton-living-history-festival-at-the-offas-dyke-centre/

[15] https://offaswatsdyke.wordpress.com/2019/09/29/opening-the-offas-dyke-association-50th-anniversary-exhibition-and-heritage-walk-at-trefonen/

Figure 16: The Offa's Dyke Journal logo by Howard Williams, adapting the design of Jonathan Felgate for the Collaboratory (Figure 7)

Association) to create a detailed and critical evaluation of the future of Offa's Dyke as an ancient monument. Now completed, the plan identifies the state of the monument and recommendations for its future conservation (Haygarth Berry Associates 2018). There is now the potential to extend this initiative to Wat's Dyke and other linear monuments in the Anglo-Welsh borderlands (D. McGlade pers. comm.).

Conservation work needs to be done proactively, and issues that were outlined in the CMP need to be addressed. In order to make a positive impact upon conservation, the ODA have taken the step to introduce the Offa's Dyke Walker's passport scheme.[16] The passport encourages walkers to obtain stamps from twelve stamping station boxes, which are only open between May and October, by encouraging walking between these months it is hoped will reduce the wear and tear and erosion that is exaggerated during the wetter winter months.

Recognition must also be given to a further initiative: the CoSMM project (Community Stewardship of Mercian Monuments).[17] This is a crowd-sourced research initiative aimed at working at a community level up and down the Anglo-Welsh border. There is palpable untapped potential for this broader network to create active local engagements with Offa's Dyke, Wat's Dyke and the various short linear earthworks found across mid-Wales and western Britain more broadly, and provide a model for community-based research elsewhere. The Collaboratory wishes to support this initiative.

Moreover, the Collaboratory aims to create synergies with the revitalised and fresh initiatives for public engagement taken forward by the Offa's Dyke Association, with a rich set of resources on its website[18] and social media presence via Twitter[19] and Facebook.[20]

The Offa's Dyke Journal

In addition to the creation of online resources, including a blog and a host of activities and events, a further initiative of the Collaboratory was to establish a research venue to collate and disseminate key past studies of frontiers and borderland monuments and landscapes, as well as to provide a high-quality peer-reviewed venue to provide readily accessible venue for new research (Figure 16). Published in collaboration with JAS Arqueología and funded by the University of Chester and the Offa's Dyke Association,[21] the *Journal* has its own digital publishing platform.[22] *Offa's Dyke Journal* is thus not only a free, open-source venue for research but also it is at the forefront of the field initiative to create an annual publication of high-quality research promoting cross-disciplinary discourse beyond the remit of other journals. Hence, the *Journal* plans to incorporate research investigating dimensions of Offa's Dyke, Wat's Dyke and the short dykes of western Britain, including their life-histories and landscape contexts, but also investigations of frontiers and borderlands from elsewhere in Britain, Europe and beyond from prehistory to the contemporary world. Moreover, we do not wish to emphasise just the monuments themselves or the visions and realities of their design and implementation, but also their use, abandonment and reuse. Integral to this work is considering active and passive resistances to linear monuments and the wider networks of control and surveillance associated with them. In this regard, we aspire for the *Journal* to explore mobility in terms of control, but also in terms of its subversion.

A further dimension of the *Journal* that deserves mention is the character of its production. As primarily a digital venue, we have worked hard to foster tabular and figural support for the contents in a fashion unrivalled by many traditional studies of linear monuments and their landscapes. These include tables, maps, colour photographs and diagrams to help explain the complex and often ephemeral character of the sites and monuments under investigation. Too often, even archaeological and landscape studies leave the readers unclear regarding the scale and character of their discoveries.

While there are plenty of venues to publish research on the archaeology, history and heritage of frontiers and borderlands, few consistently incorporate a deep-time focus on material culture, monumentality and landscape in equal measure. Certainly, one of the recognised problems with existing venues is over-respect towards regional and national borders, with Wat's Dyke and Offa's Dyke, as well as the shorter linear earthworks of the Anglo-Welsh borderlands, suffering from being treated and considered simply as fragments straddling modern political and administrative boundaries. For early medieval linear earthworks, the literature has been sporadic, appearing in diverse venues such as county and regional journals, as well as national and international themed and period specific journals. As mentioned above, Offa's Dyke itself has only received four book-length studies (Fox 1955;

Noble 1983; Hill and Worthington 2003; Ray and Bapty 2016), the first two of which have long been out of print. Meanwhile, broader studies of linear earthworks have been sparse too (but see Bell 2012; Grigg 2018). Looking farther afield in geographical terms, there exist no multi-period journals dedicated to frontier and borderlands, including studies of the design, development, afterlives and landscape contexts of frontier work. Hence, notwithstanding the specific needs for the Anglo-Welsh borderlands, the Offa's Dyke fills an important niche for European and global studies of frontiers and borderlands from prehistory to the present.

The first two volumes of the *Journal* will be initially co-edited by Howard Williams and doctoral researcher Liam Delaney (both of the University of Chester), but the editorial composition may well evolve with subsequent volumes in response to the other commitments and priorities of the convenors and members of the Collaboratory. Its editorial board comprises the convenors of the Collaboratory with the invited addition of further individuals with disciplinary, thematic and geographical research expertise pertinent to the aspired scope of the *Journal*. As with the editorial responsibilities, we are looking to augment the Board through subsequent issues with individuals offering further relevant expertise and perspectives.

The Journal's name

In this light, we must say a word about the title of the journal, which might at a first glance be seen as valorising the exceptionalism attributed to Offa's Dyke, and together with this the focus on the rulers and builders as opposed to those affected by their construction. To avoid this, one option was to select a geographically and temporally neutral thematic title such as 'Journal of Frontier Studies in Archaeology, History and Heritage'. However, it was felt such a title might be overly ambitious, inevitably misleading and cumbersome, as well as failing to articulate both the early medieval and the Anglo-Welsh borderlands foci of the initial venture. Moreover, the terms 'frontier' and 'border/borderlands' are frequently deployed in different fashions across and within disciplines, giving a geographical and material focus retains flexibility in the scope of contributions, rather than restricting it. The *Offa's Dyke Journal* thus creates and affords the cross-disciplinary intellectual space for ongoing debates about the terminology and significance of frontiers and borderlands, including those traversing and inhabiting them past and present.

We wish the *Journal* to be considered open to original contributions offering fresh theories, methods and data in the comparative and interdisciplinary study of frontiers and borderlands. Hence, as with the Collaboratory, the 'Offa's Dyke' of our title is a lens through which all frontiers and borderlands, great or small, past or present, might be considered afresh and from interdisciplinary perspectives. The 'Offa's Dyke' of our title is thus an archaic allusion and intellectual focus, rather than a strict description of the *Journal*'s primary subject matter. In other words, the title uses Britain's longest linear earthwork as an iconic focus for a venue that seeks to explore afresh different linear earthworks and other frontier works in comparative terms, from prehistory to the present, and across the globe.

The Sponsors

The Department of History and Archaeology is one of many academic departments at the University of Chester which has long fostered engagement with the built and natural environment. The Department's staff have a rich track record of public engagement and institutional collaboration within the city of Chester, the county of Cheshire and neighbouring counties and regions, including communities and stakeholders on both sides of the modern Anglo-Welsh border. The University of Chester, through the auspices of the generous support of the Faculty of Arts and Humanities, thus provides an appropriate and fitting sponsor for this new venture. Specifically, the *Journal* answers the University's vision to grow scholarship and research, as well as to engender pride and shared ownership in its endeavours. Specifically, the *Journal* maps onto the University's foundational values to apply academic knowledge and skills to benefit in the regions it represents, and foster well-being and creativity for all, in this instance through an appreciation and engagement with the historic environment.[23]

Sponsorship by the University of Chester is matched by the Offa's Dyke Association, a volunteer-led organisation who manage the Offa's Dyke Centre.[24] They are not only facilitating and sustaining the online journal's creation but also plan to promote the dissemination of the *Journal* through its sale at the Offa's Dyke Centre in Knighton, Powys: the only visitor centre associated with any of Britain's long-distance footpaths. Furthermore, we are proud and pleased that the *Journal* is to be launched to coincide with the 50th anniversary year of the Association and hope that its members might regard it as long overdue academic recognition of their long-standing and dedicated endeavours to promote both Offa's Dyke and the Offa's Dyke Path National Trail. From this perspective, it is clear that Offa's Dyke Association, which in response to the research of the Offa's Dyke Collaboratory has extended its charitable aims to encapsulate Wat's Dyke and the Wat's Dyke Way,[25] is also supporting academic research and public engagement as well as many important conservation initiatives for the path and the monument. Offa's Dyke and Wat's Dyke are thus increasingly appreciated as only of interest and benefit to long-distance walkers and local communities, they have stories and significance to tell about the past and present frictions and fables, flaws and follies, of marking, building and using boundaries as borders which are of global import.

Reviewing volume 1

In addition to this Introduction, the first volume of the *Offa's Dyke Journal* contains six articles. Two are 'classics revisited' contributions: by Ann Williams and Margaret Worthington Hill. Meanwhile, four are original peer-reviewed articles: by Paul Belford, Andy Seaman, Astrid Tummmuscheit and Frauke Witte, and John Swogger.

---

[23]   https://www1.chester.ac.uk/about/the-university/our-mission-vision-and-values
[24]   https://offasdyke.org.uk/offas-dyke-association/
[25]   https://www.watsdykeway.com/

We start with a re-titled, re-formatted and revised version of a relatively recent publication. Ann Williams published her 'Offa's Dyke: a monument without a history' in 2009 in an edited collection tackling the history of fortified borders: *Walls, Ramparts, and Lines of Demarcation: Selected Studies from Antiquity to Modern Times* (Williams 2009). Ten years on, this chapter merits a broader audience through open-access digital publication, providing as it does a much-needed and critical review of the scant and problematic historical evidence for Offa's Dyke. In the newly titled 'Offa's Dyke: 'the Stuff that Dreams are Made of' Williams has worked hard with the journal editors to update her research, published here with the blessings and support of her former editors. Moreover, the article originally appeared without illustrations, potentially restricting the article's ability to present the monument's form and character to those unfamiliar with it. The new version of the article appears with much-needed visual support, namely ground-level photographs and drone photographic images, as well as a map of the monument designed and created by Liam Delaney showing the current presumed route of Offa's Dyke from the Wye Valley (Gloucestershire) to Treuddyn (Flintshire). As it now appears, the article provides a valuable introduction to both the historical evidence and the material form of Offa's Dyke. Williams challenges us not to be so confident in our estimation of precise political and administrative contexts for the building of the Dyke, but to consider its potential significances beyond 'purpose', thus providing an essential foundation for fresh work on linear earthworks and other lines of borders and frontier works in other times and places as extending beyond the motives of their makers.

Next, we have a second 'classic revisited' article, namely Margaret Worthington Hill's 1997 'Wat's Dyke: An Archaeological and Historical Enigma', originally appearing in a special guest-edited issue of the *Bulletin of the John Rylands Library* edited by Gale Owen-Crocker called *Anglo-Saxon Texts and Contexts*. At the time of its publication, this was the only significant piece of work on Wat's Dyke since Sir Cyril Fox's field survey (Fox 1934; 1955). Wat's Dyke has been repeatedly side-lined and overlooked by subsequent researchers (but see Malim and Hayes 2008; Ray and Bapty 2016). Worthington Hill was writing before radiocarbon and OSL dating of Wat's Dyke at Gobowen to the early ninth century, thus suggesting Wat's Dyke was a *successor* monument to Offa's Dyke, rather than a predecessor as many had speculated (Malim and Hayes, contra Fox 1955; Hill and Worthington 2003). Hence, the article might be superficially dismissed as now out-of-date for continuing to favour a view of Wat's Dyke as pre-Offan. However, her review, based on sustained fieldwork, demonstrated the integrity of the linear earthwork from Basingwerk in Flintshire south to Maesbury and perhaps beyond. Therefore it is an important statement regarding the continuous and coherent monumentality of its design and construction, which Fox (1955) had already considered as comparable to Offa's Dyke in form if not overall length. Likewise, Worthington Hill's documentary research drew a key observation from the relationship between the line of Wat's Dyke and hidated and unhidated manors recorded in Domesday Book, the former to the Dyke's eastern (Mercian) side, the latter to the western (Welsh) side. If we now read Worthington Hill's article in relation to Malim and Hayes' (2008) research on dating

Wat's Dyke, we can underscore the notion that Wat's Dyke might have been built to face a unified opponent and may have had a more enduring legacy through the ninth, tenth and eleventh centuries in this borderland landscape than its Offan predecessor. The original article was again supported by few illustrations; a key contribution of this re-publication is not only to make it available to new audiences via open-access digital publication, but also to enhance the visual character of the article's argumentation. Here, the study is supported not only by Worthington Hill's original two maps, but also by photographs by Howard Williams showing the Dyke's present-day condition as it passes through farmland, woodland and suburbs. Furthermore, thanks to a CPAT photograph taken by Chris Musson, identified and supplied by Gary Duckers (Clwyd-Powys HER), Worthington Hill's arguments regarding the southern extent of Wat's Dyke are afforded additional support. Future research will benefit considerably from this revised and enhanced version of the article.

Complementing this pair of re-published articles, Paul Belford presents and contextualises the interim results of recent archaeological investigations on the pair of linear earthworks in Wrexham county borough, each within the present-day grounds of National Trust properties. The excavations at Wat's Dyke close to Erddig Hall, and Offa's Dyke at Chirk Castle were conducted by Clwyd-Powys Archaeological Trust. The quality of the fieldwork is notable given how few previous investigations of either monument in cross-section have revealed both bank and ditch together and have effectively followed the ditch down to a demonstrable and convincing base. The inclusion of community volunteers on both projects within landscapes which are popular destinations for tourists and locals alike is a further notable feature of the work. Regarding the nature of the archaeology itself, the excavations revealed in detail the nature of these monuments through systematic small-scale investigation (Belford this volume). Notably, it revealed how both bank and ditch could survive in locations outside of scheduled areas and where surface traces are limited. A further key point is that, in each excavation is that underlying and thus earlier archaeological features were found which might help with dating the monuments and identifying prior land uses.

The fourth article, the second original contribution, tackles a different landscape, but one also closely bound up with the conflicts between the early medieval Mercian and Welsh kingdoms. Rather than their military or territorial role, Andy Seaman focuses on the myths and legends that might have accrued around linear earthworks in politically contested early medieval central place zones. The dyke of Llywarch Hen is the focus of Andy Seaman's article, a 4km-long head dyke that framed the eastern approaches to the royal estate of Llan-gors. The crannog upon the lake to its west has been archaeologically was proved to be a royal site of the Kingdom of Brycheiniog, and Seaman reflects on the role of the dyke in accruing legendary associations, mobilising ancient heroes as ideological tools of political legitimisation in the landscape. Seaman contextualises his argument in relation to other 'short dykes' of the Anglo-Welsh borderland which might have also had both territorial and mnemonic significances, suggesting that histories and mythologies were layered via oral and literary traditions in the early medieval landscape setting. This argument has significant and far-reaching implications for considering the names attributed to other dykes across Britain, including Wansdyke, Wat's Dyke and Offa's Dyke. Place-names associated with linear earthworks might give us more and different information than the names of their supposed builders: they might constitute enduring ideological discourses on landscape and memory in their own right.

The *Offa's Dyke Journal* seeks not only to explore linear earthworks in Wales and England, but to provide a venue for comparative studies, past and present, from across Europe and the globe. It is to the Continent that we next turn, and the third original article constitutes a valuble English-language summary of the recent fieldwork conducted along the complex of linear earthworks known collectively as the Danevirke. Tummuscheit and Witte provide a new set of dates and a revitalised sequence for this important set of monuments which evolved to control maritime transportation across, and land routes through, the stem of the Jutlandic peninsula. Thanks to their work, we have a better understanding of the monumental biography of these linear features. Moreover, having achieved UNESCO World Heritage Site status in 2018, the Danevirke is now telling a story on a global scale regarding how linear monuments can be used and reused, extended and augmented, accruing and shifting its function and significance for almost two millennia from at least the 2nd century AD to the present day. The eighth-century phase was incomparable on mainland Europe, and its parallels, and differences, with linear earthworks in Britain are ripe for revaluation.

It should be clear from the contents reviewed thus far that the *Journal* sees not only to publish past and fresh research on frontiers and borderlands, but also to provide a venue for critical evaluation of how we engage audiences in their stories in the contemporary world. Our fourth original article is by archaeologist and artist John G. Swogger: drawing on his worldwide experience at the intersection of art and archaeology, he presents the particular changes of visualising linear earthworks for present-day heritage contexts using comics as a medium. As part of his *Oswestry Heritage Comics*, the linear earthworks of Offa's Dyke and Wat's Dyke have been visualised in different ways as part of a kaleidoscope of localised narratives linking past and present. As Swogger shows, his work provides a model for potential future work in a host of media, and the digital age encourages us to think about site- and landscape-based interpretation, but also online media to engage audiences globally in the comparative and rich stories of frontiers and borderlands.

The future

By setting this up as an annual *Journal* disseminated primarily via digital means, the Collaboratory is making a bold and ambitious statement about creating a cross-disciplinary research focus for the medium and long term. This does not mean the *Offa's Dyke Journal* will run in perpetuity. It's editorial team and Board, foci, character, venue and title may, and perhaps should, continually shift and evolve. Indeed, we recognise that while our aim will be to create a resource of lasting value to academics and the public, we might not be able to sustain annual publications indefinitely.

Conclusion

> ...barriers do not necessarily mark, or help to defend, boundaries between powers. Still, we know that some borders might become highly charged with symbolic meanings. Thus the frontier between Franks and (Avar or Magyar) 'Huns' was not only a dividing line between Christians and pagans, but could come to be regarded as a border between good and evil, salvation and apocalypse altogether. (Pohl 2005: 257)

This introduction to the first volume of the *Offa's Dyke* journal has established the multidisciplinary necessity of this new publication venue, its character and foci. We have also reviewed the content of the first volume and identified the potential for future submissions.

It is our belief that linear monuments and their landscapes offer relatively untapped potential for both fresh research and public engagement in the past and present significance of frontiers and borderlands. Linear earthworks are deceptive. They are seemingly very simple monuments – conservatively described as a bank and ditch earthwork built between two locations – yet they conceal a vast amount of information about the past. Not only can the design of form of dykes be much more nuanced but individualistic differences to each monument can reveal hints to their construction and their purpose. Additionally, by studying their route and placement in the landscape, the agency behind their construction can be discerned. The time and labour invested in creating and maintain such monuments might reveal rich details about the politics, state control and the anxieties of that state – themes revealed in contemporary historical and archaeological evidence of other forms. Further still, these features do not just reveal aspects on the states that constructed them, but the societies and communities that these frontier monuments were built against, and these can often be completely invisible to our surviving historical records.

It is our hope that this journal can be a suitable venue to promote research which has largely struggled to find a place in archaeological narratives of landscape history. These earthworks are some of the largest earthworks in Europe and it is our hope that this journal can help to put them back in the historical landscape and, colloquially, use these boundary features to build research bridges.

We envisaged this journal to be at its core both digital and open source, meaning it has the largest possibility to be as accessible and as available to researchers as possible. This was achieved whilst equally providing unbiased cutting-edge new research and availability of now difficult to access articles. It should be a venue for a wide range of topics, from a wide range of researchers and it is their hope that this vision continues.

Looking forward to the future; we welcome submissions and notifications of interest for future issues. The deadline for papers to be submitted for volume 2 is currently set at 1 May 2020 and we look forward to a rich and diverse set of contributions in future issues.

Acknowledgements

This *Journal* would not have been possible without the editor of the Offa's Dyke Collaboratory's convenors, members and the *Journal*'s editorial board. Thanks to the University of Chester and the Offa's Dyke Association for continued support, JAS Arqueologia for taking on this *Journal* to publication, and to Jonathan Felgate for designing the Collaboratory logo which in turn inspired the *Journal*'s. Thanks also to Jaima Almánsa Sanchez, Tim Grady and Adam Parsons for constructive input on the design of the *Journal*. Earlier drafts of this benefited from the helpful comments of Paul Belford, Kara Critchell and Clare Downham. Pauline Clarke proof-read the entire first volume and we thank her for attention to detail and constructive observations.

Bibliography

Alibaigi, S. 2019. The Gawri Wall: a possible Partho-Sasanian structure in the western foothills of the Zagros Mountains. *Antiquity* 93(370): 1–8.

Allen, D. 1988. Excavations on Offa's Dyke, Ffrydd Road, Knighton, Powys, 1976. *Radnorshire Society Transactions* 58, 7–10.

Bapty, I. 2004. The final word on Offa's Dyke? Clwyd-Powys Archaeological Trust website viewed 29 March 29 2019, www.cpat.org.uk/offa/offrev.htm

Baker, J. and Brookes, S. 2015. Explaining Anglo-Saxon military efficiency: the landscape of mobilization. *Anglo-Saxon England* 44: 221–258.

Bartlett, R. and MacKay, A. (eds) 1989. *Medieval Frontier Societies.* Oxford: Clarendon Press.

Belford, P. 2017. Offa's Dyke: a line in the landscape, in T. Jenkins and R. Abbiss (eds) *Fortress Salopia.* Solihull: Helion: 60–81.

Bell, M. 2012. *The Archaeology of the Dykes: From the Roman to Offa's Dyke.* Stroud: Amberley.

Bennett, R., Welham, K., Hill, R.A. and Ford, A. 2013. Using lidar as part of a multi-sensor approach to archaeological survey and interpretation, in R. Opitz and D, Cowley (eds) *Interpreting Archaeological Topography: Airborne Laser Scanning, 3D Data and Ground Observation.* Aerial Archaeology Research Group 5: 197–205.

Boozer, A. 2018. The archaeology of Imperial borderlands, in B. Düring and T. Stek (eds) *The Archaeology of Imperial Landscapes: A Comparative Study of Empires in the Ancient Near East and Mediterranean World.* Cambridge: Cambridge University Press: 206–239.

Bowen, H.C. 1990. *The Archaeology of Bokerley Dyke*. Norwich: Stationery Office Books.

Brather, S. 2005. Acculturation and ethnogenesis along the frontier: Rome and the Ancient Germans in an archaeological perspective, in F. Curta (ed.) *Borders, Barriers, and Ethnogenesis. Frontiers in Late Antiquity and the Middle Ages*. Turnhout: Brepols: 139–172.

Breeze, D. 2018. The value of studying Roman frontiers. *Theoretical Roman Archaeology Journal* 1(1), DOI: http://doi.org/10.16995/traj.212

Brookes, S. 2013. Mapping Anglo-Saxon civil defence, in J. Baker, S. Brookes and A. Reynolds (eds) *Landscapes of Defence in Early Medieval Europe*, Turnhout: Brepols: 39–63.

Collins, R. 2012. *Hadrian's Wall and the End of Empire. The Roman Frontier in the 4th and 5th Centuries*. London: Routledge.

Curta, F. 2005. Introduction, in F. Curta (ed.) *Borders, Barriers, and Ethnogenesis. Frontiers in Late Antiquity and the Middle Ages*. Turnhout: Brepols: 1–9.

DeAtley, S.P. and Findlow, F.J. 1984. *Exploring the Limits: Frontiers and Boundaries in Prehistory*. Oxford: British Archaeological Repots International Series 223.

Dobat, A.S. 2008. Danevirke revisited: an investigation into military and socio-political organisation in south Scandinavia (c. 700 to 1100). *Medieval Archaeology* 52: 27–67.

Edwards, N. 2009. Re-thinking the Pillar of Eliseg. *Antiquaries Journal* 89: 143–177.

Erskine, J.G.P. 2007. The West Wansdyke: an appraisal of the dating, dimensions and construction techniques in the light of excavated evidence. *Archaeological Journal* 164: 80–108.

Everson, P. 1991. Three case studies of ridge and furrow: 1. Offa's Dyke at Dudston in Chirbury, Shropshre. A pre-Offan field system? *Landscape History* 13(1): 53–63.

Fauser, M., Friedrichs, A and Harders, L. 2019. Migrations and borders: practices and politics of inclusion and exclusion in Europe from the nineteenth to the twenty-first century. *Journal of Borderlands Studies* 34(4): 483–488.

Flynn, D.K. 2008. 'We are the border': identity, exchange, and the state along the Bénin-Nigeria border. *American Ethnologist* 24(2): 311–330

Fox, C. 1934. Wat's Dyke: a field survey. *Archaeologia Cambrensis* 90: 205–278.

Fox, C. 1955. *Offa's Dyke. A Field Survey of the Western Frontier-Works of Mercia in the Seventh and Eighth Centuries A.D.* London: The British Academy/Oxford University Press.

Fox, A. and Fox, C. 1958. Wansdyke reconsidered. *Archaeological Journal* 115: 1–48.

Fryde, N. and Reitz, D. (eds) 2009. *Walls, Ramparts, and Lines of Demarcation: Selected Studies from Antiquity to Modern Times*. Munster: LIT Verlag Munster.

Gelling, M. 1992. *The West Midlands in the Early Middle Ages*. Leicester: Leicester University Press.

Grigg, E. 2014. The early medieval dykes of Britain, in G.R. Owen-Crocker and S.D. Thompson (eds) *Towns and Topography: Essays in Memory of David M. Hill*. Oxford: Oxbow: 103–110.

Grigg, E. 2018. *Warfare, Raiding and Defence in Early Medieval Britain.* Ramsbury: Robert Hale.

Hamilakis, Y. (ed.) 2018. *The New Nomadic Age: Archaeologies of Forced and Undocumented Migration.* Sheffield: Equinox.

Hankinson, R. and Caseldine, A. 2006. Short dykes in Powys and their origins. *Archaeological Journal* 163: 264–269.

Hannon, N. 2018. *The Hidden Landscape of a Roman Frontier: A LiDAR survey of the Antonine Wall, World Heritage Site.* Canterbury Christ Church University: Thesis submitted for the Degree of Doctor of Philosophy.

Hardt, M. 2005. The *Limes Saxoniae* as part of the eastern borderlands of the Frankish and Ottonian-Salian Empire, in F. Curta (ed.) *Borders, Barriers, and Ethnogenesis. Frontiers in Late Antiquity and the Middle Ages.* Turnhout: Brepols: 35–49.

Haygarth Berry Associates 2018. *Offa's Dyke Conservation Management Plan.* Draft 30 November 2018. Offa's Dyke Association.

Hesse, R. 2013. The changing picture of archaeological landscapes: lidar prospection over very large areas as part of a cultural heritage strategy, in R. Opitz and D. Cowley (eds) *Interpreting Archaeological Topography: Airborne Laser Scanning, 3D Data and Ground Observation.* Aerial Archaeology Research Group 5: 171–184.

Hill, D. 1974. The inter-relation of Offa's and Wat's dykes. *Antiquity* 48: 309–312.

Hill, D. 1991. Offa and Wat's Dykes, in J. Manley, S. Grenter and F. Gale (eds) *The Archaeology of Clwyd.* Clwyd Archaeological Service, Denbigh: Clwyd County Council: 142–156.

Hill, D. 2000. Offa's Dyke, pattern and purpose. *Antiquaries Journal* 80: 195–206.

Hill, D. 2001. Mercians: the dwellers on the boundary, in M.P. Brown and C.A. Farr (eds) *Mercia: An Anglo-Saxon Kingdom in Europe.* Leicester: Leicester University Press: 173–182.

Hill, D. and Worthington, M. 2003. *Offa's Dyke: History and Guide.* Stroud: Tempus.

Hingley, R. 2008. Hadrian's Wall in theory: pursuing new agendas, in P. Bidwell (ed.) *Understanding Hadrian's Wall.* Kendal: The Arbeia Society: 25–28

Hingley, R. 2012. *Hadrian's Wall: A Life.* Oxford: Oxford University Press.

Konrad, V. and Brunet-Jailly, E. 2019. Approaching borders, creating borderland spaces, and exploring the evolving borders between Canada and the United States. *The Canadian Geographer* 63(1): 4–10

Ladd, S. and Mortimer, R. 2017. The Bran Ditch: Early Iron Age origins and implications for prehistoric territories in South Cambridgeshire and the East Chilterns. *Proceedings of the Cambridge Antiquarian Society* 106: 7–22.

Lennon, B. 2010. The relationship between Wansdyke and Bedwyn Dykes: a historiography. *Wiltshire Archaeological and Natural History Magazine* 103: 269–288.

Lewis, J. 2012. Borders in a limestone landscape Neolithic cave use in the Mendip Hills South-West England, in D. Mullin (ed.) *Places in Between: The Archaeology of Social, Cultural and Geographic*

Borders and Borderlands. Oxford: Oxbow: 48–57.

Maldonado, A. 2015. The early medieval Antonine Wall. *Britannia* 46: 225–245.

Malim, T. with Penn, K., Robinson, B., Wait, G. and Welsh, K. 1997. New evidence on the Cambridgeshire dykes and Worsted Street Roman Road. *Proceedings of the Cambridge Antiquarian Society* 85: 27–122.

Malim, T. and Hayes, L. 2008. The date and nature of Wat's Dyke: a reassessment in the light of recent investigations at Gobowen, Shropshire, in S. Crawford and H. Hamerow (eds) *Anglo-Saxon Studies in Archaeology and History* 15. Oxford: Oxbow: 147–79.

Malim, T. 2007. The origins and design of linear earthworks in the Welsh Marches. *Landscape Enquires, Proceedings of the Clifton Antiquarian Club* 8: 13–32.

McAtackney, L. 2015. Memorials and marching: archaeological insights into segregation in contemporary Northern Ireland. *Historical Archaeology* 49(3): 110–125.

McWilliams, A. 2013. *An Archaeology of the Iron Curtain.* Stockholm: Södertörn.

Mullin, D. 2011a. Border crossings. The archaeology of borders and borderlands, in D. Mullin (ed.) *Places in Between: The Archaeology of Social, Cultural and Geographical Borders and Borderlands,* Oxford: Oxbow: 1–12.

Mullin, D. 2011b. Towards an archaeology of borders and borderlands, in D. Mullin (ed.) *Places in Between: The Archaeology of Social, Cultural and Geographical Borders and Borderlands.* Oxford: Oxbow: 99–104.

Murray, J. 2018. *A GIS-based Analysis of Hillfort Location and Morphology.* Oxford: British Archaeological Series 644.

Murrieta-Flores, P. and Williams, H. 2017. Placing the Pillar of Eliseg: movement, visibility and memory in the early medieval landscape. *Medieval Archaeology* 61(1), 69–103.

New Forest Heritage. 2018. *Heritage Mapping.* New Forest National Park Authority, viewed 5 June 2019: http://www.newforestheritage.org/

Noble, F. 1983. *Offa's Dyke Reviewed.* Oxford: British Archaeological Reports British Series, 114.

O' Drisceoil, C., Leenane, M., Davis, S., Fitzgibbon, B. and Teehan M. 2014. *The Black Pig's Dyke Regional Project 2014.* Monaghan: Heritage Council of Ireland.

Pohl, W. 2005. Frontiers and ethnic identities: some final considerations, in F. Curta (ed.) *Borders, Barriers, and Ethnogenesis. Frontiers in Late Antiquity and the Middle Ages.* Turnhout: Brepols: 255–65.

Rahtz, P. 1961. An excavation on Bokerly Dyke, 1958. *Archaeological Journal* 118(1): 65–99.

Ravest, J. 2019. Offa's Dyke by Drone, Paper presented at the Offa's Dyke Association 50th Anniversary Weekend, Offa's Dyke Centre Knighton, 5 May 2019.

Ray, K. and Bapty, I. 2016. *Offa's Dyke: Landscape and Hegemony in Eighth-Century Britain.* Oxford: Windgather Press.

Reynolds, A. 2013. Archaeological correlates for Anglo-Saxon military activity in comparative perspective, in J. Baker, S. Brookes and A. Reynolds (eds) *Landscapes of Defence in Early Medieval Europe*, Turnhout: Brepols: 1–38.

Reynolds, A. and Langlands, A. 2006. Social identities on the macro scale: a maximum view of Wansdyke, in W. Davies, G. Halsall, and A. Reynolds (eds) *People and Space in the Middle Ages 300–1300*, Studies in the Early Middle Ages 15, Turnhout: Brepols: 13–44.

Tyler, D.J. 2011. Offa's Dyke: an historiographical appraisal. *Journal of Medieval History* 37(2): 145–161.

Squatriti, P. 2002. Digging ditches in Early Medieval Europe. *Past and Present* 175: 11–65.

Squatriti, P. 2004. Offa's Dyke between nature and culture. *Environmental History* 9: 9–36.

Squatriti, P. 2006. Moving earth and making difference: dikes and frontiers in early medieval Bulgaria, in F. Curta (ed.) *Borders, Barriers, and Ethnogenesis. Frontiers in Late Antiquity and the Middle Ages*. Turnhout: Brepols: 59–90.

Swallow, R. 2016. Cheshire castles of the Irish Sea cultural zone. *Archaeological Journal* 173: 288–341.

Wileman, J. 2003. The purpose of the dykes: understanding the linear earthworks of early medieval Britain. *Landscapes* 4(2): 59–66.

Williams, A. 2009. Offa's Dyke: A Monument Without a History? in N. Fryde and D. Reitz (eds) *Walls, Ramparts, and Lines of Demarcation: Selected Studies from Antiquity to Modern Times*. Munster. LIT Verlag Munster: 31–56.

Worthington, M. 1997. Wat's Dyke: An Archaeological and Historical Enigma. *Bulletin of the John Rylands University Library of Manchester* 79(3): 177–96.

Worthington Hill, M. and Grigg, E. 2015. Boundaries and walls, in M. C. Hyer and G. R. Owen-Crocker (eds) *The Material Culture of the Built Environment in the Anglo-Saxon World*. Liverpool: Liverpool University Press: 162–181.

Howard Williams, Professor of Archaeology, Department of History and Archaeology, University of Chester, Parkgate Road, Chester CH1 4BJ, UK
Email: howard.williams@chester.ac.uk

Liam Delaney, Doctoral Researcher, Department of History and Archaeology, University of Chester, Parkgate Road, Chester CH1 4BJ, UK
Email: 1816919@chester.ac.uk

OFFA'S DYKE JOURNAL 1 2019, 32–57

Offa's Dyke: 'the Stuff that Dreams are Made of'

Ann Williams

Offa's Dyke has been much discussed in the past, and will no doubt continue to fascinate future archaeologists and historians. This article summarises the few historical sources for the Dyke which are available. It also explores the archaeological investigations which have taken place up to the time of writing in 2009.

Keywords: Asser, Mercia, Offa, Offa's Dyke, Wales, Wat's Dyke, Whitford Dyke

This article is based on a paper delivered at a conference on boundaries, held at the Technical University of Darmstadt in 2005; a date seared into my memory because my flight to Frankfurt took place on the same day as the bombing of the London Underground on the 7 July. Since the subject of the conference concerned matters of security and defence, this seems, in retrospect, rather appropriate, though at the time it was merely terrifying. The paper which I gave was subsequently published in the conference proceedings in 2009 (Fryde and Reitz 2009). The frontiers studied ranged from Britain to China, and from Antiquity to the twenty-first century, including *inter alia* the Roman Limes, the *Danevirke* (Niels Lund), the Great Wall of China, the Maginot Line, and the Berlin Wall, so that each contributor concentrated on presenting the essentials of their topic rather than attempting in-depth studies. My brief was Offa's Dyke (Figures 1–3), and since I am an historian, not an archaeologist, I spent most of the time on collecting and discussing the references to the Dyke in the medieval sources; I did not, however, survey the work of the antiquarian writers from the fifteenth century to the nineteenth (Ray and Bapty 2016: 57–66). Written references to the Dyke are not abundant. The earliest mention of what is assumed to be Offa's Dyke dates from a century after its presumed construction, and it is not even called 'Offa's Dyke' until the twelfth century. This sparse historical record of what must have been a major monument is a reminder of how biased contemporary sources are towards royal and ecclesiastical affairs, with little direct reference to social and economic matters. It is this part of my paper which may still be of some interest, since I do not think that much documentary or literary evidence has subsequently emerged. Archaeological investigation of the Dyke has, on the contrary, proceeded apace, so that my attempt to survey the archaeological evidence has been overtaken by events, and can be explored via the other articles in this first volume of the *Offa's Dyke Journal*.[1]

Offa's Dyke, the great earthwork which stretches along the debateable land between England and Wales, has over the years presented both historians and archaeologists with a number of conundrums. It is difficult in the extreme to answer the questions which the existence of the Dyke raises: who ordered it to be built, for what purpose, how was the labour involved recruited and organised, and how was it used? The period to which it is

Offa's Dyke Journal volume 1 2019
Manuscript received: 02 June 2019
accepted: 12 August 2019

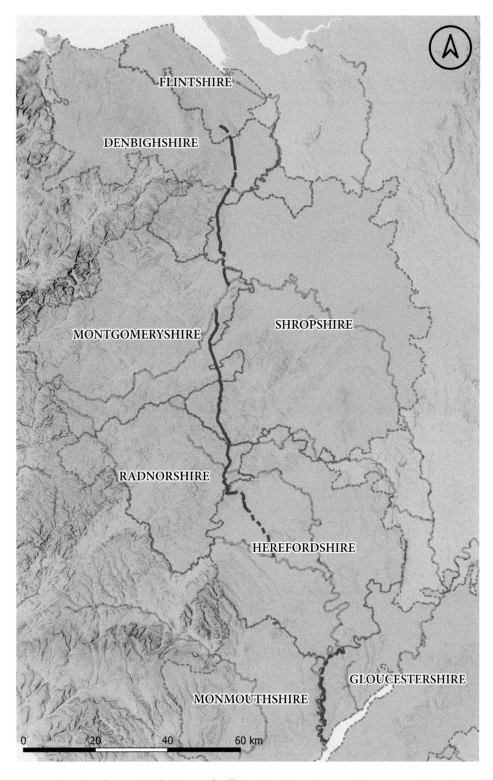

Figure 1: The established line of Offa's Dyke (Map designed by Liam Delaney)

Figure 2: Drone photograph looking north over Offa's Dyke from Llanfair Hill to Spring Hill Farm, Shropshire, showing (from left to right) the counterscarp bank to the left, the ditch, the bank and traces of quarry ditches to the right (Photograph: Julian Ravest)

attributed is one for which the historical sources, both for Wales and for England, are minimal. The archaeological record is scarcely better, since the regions which the Dyke traverses are, for the relevant period, largely aceramic and coinless, depriving us of two major means of dating the structure (Figures 2–3). Moreover, since no scrap of timber or wood has been recovered from the Dyke itself, the use of dendrochronology is precluded. The tasks of both historians and archaeologists are thus rendered even more arduous than is commonly the case. I am an historian, not an archaeologist, and my specialist field is the tenth and eleventh centuries, not the eighth and ninth. I have therefore no view of my own to present on Offa's Dyke. This may, however, be an advantage, since I also have no axe to grind. What I propose to do in this paper is lay out some of the problems which the Dyke presents, and summarise (I hope accurately) current thinking on them.

Let us begin with the sources. The scanty historical record is quickly enumerated. The earliest surviving mention of Offa's Dyke occurs in Bishop Asser's biography of King Alfred, written soon after 893, and thus a century after the death of King Offa in 796 (Keynes and Lapidge 1983: 71):

Figure 3: Drone photograph looking south from Llanfair Hill over Offa's Dyke towards Cwmsanahan Hill (Photograph: Julian Ravest)

> There was in Mercia in fairly recent times a certain vigorous king (*strenuus rex*) called Offa, who terrified all the neighbouring kings and provinces around him, and who had a great dyke (*vallum magnum*) built between Wales and Mercia from sea to sea (*de mari usque ad mare*).

Since the dating evidence is so exiguous it is perhaps worth stressing the point that it is only on the strength of Asser's words that the longest of the Dykes on the marches of England and Wales is known as Offa's Dyke.

There is no record of Offa's Dyke in Asser's main source, the *Anglo-Saxon Chronicle*, whose compilation began in King Alfred's time, and although the chronicler Æthelweard, writing in the years 978–988, describes Offa as 'a wonderful man', he does not mention Offa's Dyke (Campbell 1962: 24). The account of the Dyke in the historical collection made at the turn of the tenth and eleventh centuries by Byrhtferth of Ramsey is clearly derived from Asser (Arnold 1882: 66; Lapidge 1982: 97–122). The Dyke is not, however, mentioned by the Anglo-Norman writers of the early twelfth century (John of Worcester, William of Malmesbury, Henry of Huntingdon) who drew both on Asser and on the *Anglo-Saxon Chronicle* for much of their material. William of Malmesbury's silence is particularly remarkable, since his account of King Offa's daughter Eadburh is clearly dependent upon Asser; William echoes Asser's pejorative judgements on Eadburh and her fate (Asser's dislike arose from the marriage of Eadburh to Beorhtric of Wessex who ousted Ecgfrith, King Alfred's great-grandfather), but omits his praise for her father and his 'great dyke' (Keynes and Lapidge 1983: 71–72, 236; Mynors *et al.* 1998: 170–173). Unlike the Wansdyke in northern Wessex, Offa's Dyke does not make an impression in the estate boundaries appended to English royal diplomas. Several charters from the tenth century mention *Wodnes dic*, the Wansdyke (Sawyer 1968: nos 368, 424, 449, 647, 685, 694, 711, 777), and it may be 'the old dyke' on the boundary of Alton Priors (Wiltshire), recorded in a tenth-century will (Sawyer 1968: no 1513). In contrast to this, the only pre-Conquest charter to mention Offa's Dyke is the survey of Tidenham (Gloucestershire), which probably dates from the mid-eleventh century, and even there it appears simply as 'the dyke' (*dic*) (Sawyer 1968: no. 1555; Robertson 1956: 204–7, 451–54). One ninth-century charter does mention an *offan dic* but it cannot be Offa's Dyke, for the boundaries delineate an estate in Somerset (Sawyer 1968: no. 310). The survival of charters and diplomas, however, is linked to the presence of substantial religious establishments with the ability to make and preserve archives, and few such are to be found in the debateable lands of the Welsh marches. There are not many charters for Herefordshire, and even fewer for Shropshire and Cheshire, and many of these either have no boundary clauses, or relate to estates a few kilometres east of Offa's Dyke. The 'old dyke' (*ealdan dic*) included in the boundaries of Staunton on Arrow (Herefordshire) is the Rowe Ditch (Sawyer 1968: no 677; Finberg 1961: 141–42; Hill and Worthington 2003: 139–43).

As for the Welsh sources, if any Welsh kings issued written grants for lands in Powys, none have come down to us; the only early charter material is preserved in the twelfth-century Book of Llandaf (*Liber Landavensis*) and relates to south Wales (Davies 1982; Sims-Williams 1982: 124–29). The chief historical source, the *Annales Cambriae*, also has a south Welsh provenance; its compilation probably began at the church of St David's (Dyfed), in the early ninth century (Williams ab Ithel 1860; Winterbottom 1978; Hughes 1973: 233–58; Dumville 1977/8: 461–67). It does not, in any case, mention the Dyke. The collection of Welsh poems known as *Canu Llwyarch Hen* does refer to unnamed dykes, which may be those of Offa and Wat (Wat's Dyke runs parallel with Offa's Dyke in its northern reaches), but even if they are, the poems are no earlier than the ninth century and could be much later (Davies 1982: 210–11; Nurse 2001: 21–27).

It is not until the later twelfth and early thirteenth centuries that clear references to Offa's Dyke appear; indeed, it is only in this period that we have specific evidence that it was called 'Offa's Dyke'. In the *Vita* (life) of St Oswald, king of Northumbria (d. 642), compiled by Reginald of Durham about 1165 (Arnold 1882: 353), the battle of *Maserfeld*, in which Oswald was killed, is located by reference to 'King Offa's dyke, which divides England from North Wales' (*fossa regis Offae quae Angliam et Waliam borealem dividit*); North Wales here means Wales itself, as opposed to 'West Wales', i.e. Cornwall. Reginald adds that its purpose was to provide 'a securer bastion against his (Offa's) enemies, the Welsh' (*cuius munimine vallatus securius ab hostibus suis Walensibus*), and that it stretched 'from sea to sea'. In 1184, the Pipe Rolls, the annual records of the English Exchequer, mention a tenement called 'the fee of Offa's Dyke', lying on the boundaries of Herefordshire and Powys (Hunter 1912: 77). This is probably the tenement later known as the fee of *La Dyche*, perhaps now marked by a motte below the Dyke on the road to Evenjobb (Radnorshire) (Noble 1983: 40, 92). Walter Map, whose 'Courtiers' Trifles' (*De Nugis Curialium*) was written about 1200, says that Offa 'girdled the Welsh into a small corner of their Wales by means of the dyke which still bears his name' (James *et al.* 1923: 90–91), and in 1233, the men of Chirbury Hundred (Shropshire), who dwelt 'this side of *Offediche*' are distinguished from those who dwelt beyond it (Eyton 1860: 53).

This new interest in the Dyke in the twelfth and thirteenth centuries was perhaps sparked off by the wars of attrition which began in the eleventh century and culminated in the English conquest of Wales by Edward I. This border warfare is the context for most, if not all, the literary references to the Dyke in the twelfth and thirteenth centuries. In 1159, John of Salisbury praised the tactics of Earl Harold of Wessex, whose campaign of 1063 led to the temporary imposition of English control over the north Welsh kingdom of Gwynedd, and attributed to the victorious Harold the enactment that any Welshman found east of Offa's Dyke was to lose his right hand (Webb 1909: 19–20; Dickinson 1963: 194–95). Walter Map also records this penalty, though in his version the trespasser was to lose a foot (James *et al.* 1923: 91). As we have seen, warfare with the Welsh is also the context for the appearance of the Dyke in Reginald of Durham's life of St Oswald (Arnold 1882: 353). The idea of the Dyke as a legal and political boundary is also found in the *Description of Wales* by Gerald of Wales, completed in 1194 (Dimock 1868: 217; Thorpe 1978: 266). Gerald, like John of Salisbury, mentions Offa's Dyke in the context of Earl Harold's campaign of 1063; he celebrates Harold as the greatest of the English kings who campaigned against the Welsh, including Offa who 'shut the Welsh off from the English by his long dyke on the frontier' (*qui et fossa finali in longum extensa, Britones ab Anglis exclusivit*). Very similar is the earliest recorded appearance of Offa's Dyke in a Welsh source, the *Brut y Tywysogyon* ('Chronicle of the Kings'), which began to be compiled in the closing years of the thirteenth century (Jones 1952: xxxv–xli, 2–3; Hughes 1973: 67):

> Offa had a dyke made as a defence between him and the Welsh, so that it might be easier for him to resist the attack of his enemies. And that is called Offa's Dyke (*Clawdd Offa*) from that day to this.

The *Brut* enters the Dyke's construction under the year 798, two years after Offa's death, but the entry is probably misplaced, for Offa's demise itself is correctly entered. The comparable entry in the fifteenth-century text, *Brehinned y Saesson* ('Kings of the Saxons') also claims that the Dyke stretched 'from the one sea to the other, that is, from the South near Bristol to the North above Flint between the monastery of Basingwerk and Coleshill', thus conflating, not for the first or the last time, Offa's Dyke with Wat's (Jones, T. 1971: 10–11).

Though they cannot be regarded as reliable sources for the Dyke's original purpose and early history, what the later writers say reveals what was believed about Offa and his Dyke in their own times. Indeed, in this, as in other aspects of pre-Conquest history, twelfth-century historians set the agenda for subsequent commentators. The idea of the Dyke as the 'frontier' between England and Wales, which first appears in the twelfth century, persists to this day despite the fact that it was never the actual boundary, except briefly in the sixteenth century (Noble 1983: 75–76). The Dyke as an embattled rampart also appears most clearly in the twelfth-century texts, though the germ of this idea is contained in Asser's words. But already the Dyke was beginning to pass from history into legend. Walter Map's references to it occur in the course of a long tale about the mythical hero Gado, who allied with Offa to beat off an attack from Rome. Gado is otherwise known as Wada or Wade, after whom Wat's Dyke is thought to be named (Nurse n.d.). Since Offa's Dyke overlaps with Wat's Dyke in its northern reaches, Walter Map's association of the two as allies, though chronologically impossible (Wade, if he ever existed, belongs to the fifth century rather than the eighth) has some interest (James *et al.* 1923: 90–95; Chambers 1912: 95–103; Alexander 1966: 38, 126–27; see also Fox 1955: 288).

These brief and mostly late references constitute the historical (i.e. written) sources for Offa's Dyke. Given their exiguous nature, modern scholarship on the Dyke has concentrated on archaeological and topographical evidence. The first major investigation of Offa's Dyke, which also covered Wat's Dyke and the numerous 'short dykes' found in the same area, was that of Sir Cyril Fox (Fox 1955). In his view, the Dyke was the last and greatest in a series of attempts by the Mercians to delineate their frontier with the Welsh. The 'short dykes' were the earliest of these, perhaps constructed during the sporadic warfare between the Mercians and the men of Powys in the time of King Penda (d. 653). Next in Fox's scheme came Wat's Dyke, 'a continuous bank and ditch frontier' in the north of the border region, which he associated with the dominance of the Mercian King Æthelbald (716–57), who exercised a loose overlordship over all the English kingdoms south of the Humber. Lastly, Fox concluded, 'the final effort to define the whole western frontier of Mercia was undertaken by Offa' (Fox 1955: 285–87). Fox's interpretation of the Dyke not as a defensive or military work but as a mutually agreed frontier between Welsh and English was accepted by Sir Frank Stenton, who in his preface to Fox's book described the earthwork as 'a boundary defined by treaty or agreement between the men of the hills and the men of the lowlands' (Fox 1955: xvii; Stenton 1971: 212–15, 224). In support of his theory of a mutually agreed boundary, Stenton pointed to the existence of English place-names west of the Dyke as evidence of 'the abandonment of English territory to the Britons' (Stenton 1971: 214).

Fox's survey of the Dyke took as its starting point Asser's description of it extending 'from sea to sea', i.e., from Prestatyn, Flintshire, to Sedbury Cliff on the Severn Estuary, Gloucestershire. He explained the numerous gaps in its course in several ways. In some places the frontier was defined by rivers, notably the Severn and the Wye, 'along which an artificial line was necessary in certain places only' (Fox 1955: 277). In others notably the long stretch across the Herefordshire plain Fox postulated the existence at the time of construction of dense, damp oak-forests, which formed an impenetrable barrier between Wales and Mercia. Smaller gaps he interpreted as gateways or crossing-points, in line with his conception of the Dyke as 'not only a visible frontier but also a barrier through which lawful passage could only be attained at fixed points ... doubtless watched by frontier guards' (Fox 1955: 170).

It was the imprimatur of Sir Frank Stenton, then regarded as the final authority on the subject of English history before the Norman Conquest, which ensured that Sir Cyril Fox's opinions on Offa's Dyke became the definitive version. Not until the 1970s was another survey of the Dyke's course begun, by Frank Noble (Noble 1978). Noble died before he could complete the full realization of his research, and the section of his projected book which was in a publishable shape on his death appeared in 1983, with an introduction by Margaret Gelling (Noble 1983). This covers only the southern two-thirds of the Dyke's course (Noble 1983: vii); it is this section, however, which is least well served by Fox's examination which concentrated on the northern reaches. Noble accepted Fox's view of the Dyke as stretching 'from sea to sea', but differed from him on the details of the alignment, especially in the stretches where no obvious trace of the earthwork now exists. In particular he questioned the existence of the impenetrable oak-woods postulated by Fox to explain the gaps in the Dyke, notably in the case of the largest gap across the Herefordshire plain (Noble 1983: 18–24; Gelling 1992: 7–8, 14–19, 103–4). More fundamentally, Noble rejected the concept of the Dyke as a frontier, on the grounds that it 'did not form the actual boundary between Mercia and the independent Welsh', seeing it rather as 'a control line, a barrier set well back inside Mercian territory behind a screen of valley settlements'; the settlements are those with English place-names which Stenton interpreted as evidence of a negotiated frontier (Noble 1983: 43, 58, 75–76). The apparent gaps became, in Noble's scheme, crossing-points for legitimate traffic across the Dyke, regulated by customs similar to those recorded in the agreement known as the *Ordinance concerning the Dunsaete* (text and translation in Noble 1983: 103–109). The *Ordinance* concerns relations between Welsh and English populations on either side of a river usually identified as the Wye, though the Taradr has also been suggested as a possibility (Sims-Williams 1990: 9); it has been variously assigned to the second quarter of the tenth century and to the late tenth or early eleventh centuries (Wormald 1999: 381–82; Molyneaux 2012: 249–72).

The next investigation of the earthwork was the Offa's Dyke Project, under the direction of Professor David Hill and Margaret Worthington (Hill and Worthington 2003), whose workforce clocked up twenty-three seasons of fieldwork, excavation and surveying from a beginning in the 1970s (Hill 2000: 195–206). Among the targets of this study were the supposed gateway sites, incorporated to allow movement to and fro across the earthwork. At all the sites examined, excavation revealed the presence of the accompanying ditch, even where no trace of the bank remained. Its presence, in places some six feet (approximately 2 m) deep, argues against the incorporation of crossing-

Figure 4: Photograph of the 2014 excavations of a damaged section of Offa's Dyke by Clwyd-Powys Archaeological Trust north of Chirk (Wrexham), looking north (Reproduced courtesy of CPAT: Photo Number 3697-0066)

points in the original design, for if they had been, the ditch 'would simply not have been excavated where any gateway was needed'; rather a causeway would have been left to allow access (Hill and Worthington 2003: 91). The conclusion must be that many, if not all, of the gaps in the Dyke's course were not made in the course of its building, but are the result of later, sometimes much later destruction (but see now Ray and Bapty 2016: 228–32).

One such demolition, in the area of Knighton, Radnorshire (now Powys), took place in the 1850s and was witnessed by the historian John Earle, whose incandescent fury still burns off the pages of the report which he published in *Archaeologia Cambrensis* (Earle 1857). To quote his own words, 'it is grievous to see a noble monument like this ... allowed to fall into the power of persons who are incapable of appreciating its value, or understanding its nature'. The objects of his spleen, two brothers whom Earle contemptuously styles "men of the spade", had bought a piece of land where the Dyke crossed 'the hill top, which is called "The Ross"', at what Earle clearly considered the knock-down price of £11 an acre. When Earle arrived on the scene, they were engaged in making the former site of the Dyke 'as smooth as a garden-bed for a space of many hundred feet along the hill-slope'. On being questioned, the men responded 'We are ridding of it down, Sir', and when Earle asked them 'Why do you destroy the old dyke that has stood so many centuries?' they replied 'Oh! to make ground of it, Sir; 'tis no use as it is' (Earle 1857: 197–98). One can only sympathise with Earle's rage and second his reproachful exhortations to the comfortable worthies of Knighton, who had not come up with the money to purchase the land over which the Dyke had run, and save it from ruin. Alas, such destruction persists even in our own times (Figure 4), though nowadays archaeologists are usually able to record the details of the Dyke for posterity before the demolition men move in (see Belford (2017: 69) regarding the unauthorised damage of the Dyke at Plas Offa, Chirk, in 2013).

As well as ruling out the presence of gateways, the Offa's Dyke Project also truncated the monument's length. When the northernmost section, from Treuddyn to the Dee estuary at Prestatyn, was examined, it was discovered 'either that there are no earthworks for many miles or that where a Dyke exists, it is a separate earthwork, the Whitford Dyke, complete in itself and of a totally different construction from that in the central marches' (Hill 2000: 198). In the south too, the Offa's Dyke Project rejected all the earthworks south of Rushock Hill, Herefordshire, as integral parts of the Dyke (Hill and Worthington 2003: 129–43, 143–54). Thus redefined, Offa's Dyke 'consists of a major earthwork that runs for 103km (64 miles) from Rushock Hill [Herefordshire] to Treuddyn [Flintshire, now Clywd] … continuous except for the length along the River Severn to the north of Buttington in Montgomeryshire' (Hill and Worthington 2003: 107). It took the form of an earthen bank which still in places stands three metres high and was once perhaps twice this height, steeper on the west than on the east and accompanied on its western side by a ditch two metres deep by seven metres wide. Far from being a boundary marker, intended to regulate passage to and fro across a defined frontier, the Dyke emerges as a military and defensive structure designed to block Welsh access into Mercian territory, and following 'a carefully engineered defensive line that dominates the land to the west' (Hill and Worthington 2003: 101).

Not all Hill and Worthington's conclusions have gone unchallenged, including recent questions raised again regarding the potential presence of gateways through the Dyke (Figure 5). The exclusion of the hypothetical line northwards to the Dee estuary, and the classification of the Whitford Dyke as an unrelated monument, have not been contested to date, and it seems to be agreed by many that the numerous short lengths of earthwork across the Herefordshire Plain and in the region of English Bicknor might not be part of Offa's Dyke. It is the exclusion of the Gloucestershire earthwork, 'once continuous from Highbury in the north to Sedbury Cliff in the south', which has attracted dissent (Bapty 2004; Hare 2004: 205–6; Ray and Bapty 2016: 50–54; 89; 172–74; 275–77). One of Hill's reasons for not considering this section as part of Offa's Dyke is the existence of an eastern ditch in the stretch across St Briavels Common, whereas the main line of the Dyke has the ditch to the west. Some, however, have discerned a similar eastern ditch in sections of the main Dyke, both in Radnorshire (now Powys) and in southern Shropshire, and have argued that this is no reason to deny the inclusion of the Gloucestershire earthwork in Offa's Dyke (Bapty 2004; Ray and Bapty 2016: 82–91; 191–92: see also Fox 1955: 277) (Figure 6). Indeed, part of the Gloucestershire section is actually called *Offedich* in a deed of 1321 (Hare 2004: 206), and though this is

Figure 5: Two drone photographs of Hergan Corner (Clun Forest, Shropshire), where Offa's Dyke follows an angled turn, perhaps to assist with the surveillance and control of a possible gateway (Ray and Bapty 2016: 228–232, 237), looking south (above) and north (below) (Photographs: Julian Ravest, 2019)

Figure 6: Looking north along Offa's Dyke at Hawthorn Hill, Powys, where the ditch has long been denuded but the quarry ditch to the east of the bank is well preserved (see also Ray and Bapty 2016: 190–192). (Photograph: Howard Williams, 2019)

by no means conclusive, it should be recalled that the only pre-Conquest reference to the Dyke occurs in the survey of the Gloucestershire estate at Tidenham (Sawyer 1968: no. 1555). Perhaps we should envisage Offa building two dykes, one in southern and central Gloucestershire, the other in the central regions of the Welsh marches (Hare 2004: 206).

Having surveyed both the historical and the archaeological evidence for Offa's Dyke, it is time to try and answer some of the questions posed at the beginning of this paper: who built it, why, how was it accomplished, and how was it used? The fact that the dyke bears Offa's name is probably significant, even though the association cannot be taken back beyond the late ninth century. As Stenton observed, 'few, if any, earthworks on the scale of Offa's Dyke are associated so definitely with a particular person' (Stenton 1971: 213). Most are named, like Wat's Dyke, from mythological heroes (Offa himself, though a thoroughly historical figure, soon acquired a heroic, even a legendary aura), or from old gods, as in the case of the Wansdyke, 'Woden's dyke', and Grimsdyke, Grim, 'the hooded man', another name for Woden (in later times the Devil was, and sometimes still is held responsible for such earthworks). Offa certainly had the resources to undertake such a project, for it was in his reign (757–796) that the kingdom of the Mercians reached its political apogee. By the late 780s, all the southern English rulers acknowledged his authority; the West Saxon King Cynewulf (755–787) held out, but in 787 his successor Beorhtric married Offa's daughter Eadburh. Offa's hegemony did not extend north of the Humber, but in 792 the Northumbrian King Æthelred married Ælfflæd, Eadburh's sister. Not only did Offa have the power, he also possessed the necessary will and drive. Though it is difficult to look back through the later accretions to the real man, what little we know of him suggests towering, even over-weening ambition; when a Frankish embassy arrived in 790 requesting a daughter of Offa as a bride for the son of Charlemagne, Offa refused, unless Charlemagne's daughter Bertha was sent as the bride of his own son Ecgfrith. Not unnaturally the demand was refused, and not only did no marriage-alliance take place, but commercial relations between Frankish and English ports were temporarily suspended (Nelson 2001: 132–33).

The Frankish kingdom under Charlemagne was the model for all the emerging kingships of Western Europe, and Offa's Mercia was no exception; one of the earliest royal consecrations in English history, that of Offa's son Ecgfrith in 787 (which confirmed him as his father's successor), was inspired by the consecrations of Charlemagne's sons in 781 (Nelson 2001: 134). Frankish and English rulers of the seventh and eighth centuries drew their ideas on kingship from two sources: the image of the late Roman emperors, mediated through the Church, and the remote past of heroic saga. Both traditions, Roman and Germanic, might have provided Offa with the inspiration for a great boundary work. The physical remains of the Roman past were prestigious relics (Hunter 1974: 44, 48); when St Cuthbert visited Carlisle, for instance, the king's reeve took him on a tour of the city's walls and 'a marvellously constructed fountain of Roman workmanship' (Colgrave 1940: 123–24, 242–45). Perhaps Offa experienced similar feelings about the impressive Roman structures at Bath. A minster had been established there in the late seventh century, and in 781 Offa forced the bishop of Worcester, into whose possession the church and its lands had come, to relinquish it into his own hands (Sims-Williams 1990: 159–61). Bath's strategic position, on the frontier between Mercia and Wessex, might explain Offa's desire to control it, but the key structures were the surviving Roman buildings, celebrated in the Old English poem known as *The Ruin* (Alexander 1966: 29–31). Its provenance and date are unclear, but the author's admiration for the great works now ruined echoes the general regard for antiquity in the seventh and eighth centuries. Indeed, though it is often cited as evidence that the English feared the ruined cities as abodes of giants, its message might rather be 'come to Bath and see our splendid Roman remains'. Chief among them were the hot springs and the baths which gave the place its name. By the end of Offa's life a royal residence had been established in the city; one of the few diplomas issued in the brief reign of his son Ecgfrith (Sawyer 1968: no. 148) was enacted at 'the famous place called in the English tongue, at the Baths' (*æt Baþum*). In developing the role of Bath, Offa may have had a Frankish as well as a Roman precedent in mind, for it was in the early 790s that Charlemagne had 'begun to adopt a more sedentary life by the hot springs of Aachen' (Blair 2005: 274–75). If the Mercian rulers wished to emulate their Frankish contemporaries then Bath, with its antique architecture and hot springs, was the obvious candidate for an English Aachen. The untimely death of Ecgfrith and his replacement by a collateral line of kings meant that Bath did not develop into a Mercian capital on the lines of Aachen, though a charter of Burgred of Mercia, dated 864 (Sawyer 1968: no. 210), was issued 'at the hot baths' (æt þæm hatum baþum). It was also at Bath, variously called Baðam/Hatabaðum, and Acemannesceastre (the first element of which appears to relate to the Romano-British name Aquae Sulis), that the West Saxon king Edgar was consecrated as king of the English in 973 (Whitelock et al. 1965: Swanton 1996: 118–19).

It seems that Offa was open to both Frankish and Roman influence in his quest for the trappings of royal power. So far as the Dyke is concerned, the models might have been the greatest frontier fortifications in Offa's Britain, the walls of Hadrian and Antoninus, which had already caught the imagination of some English and British writers. In the Historia Ecclesiastica, completed in 731, Bede describes what is clearly Hadrian's Wall as 'a great ditch and a very strong rampart ... from sea to sea' (magnam fossam firmissimumque vallum ... a mari ad mare). Bede did not attribute the Wall to Hadrian, believing that the ditch and the vallum were constructed by the Emperor Severus, and that the stone wall was not added until the early fifth century (Colgrave and Mynors 1969: 26–27, 42–43); the British writer Gildas, whose work was used by Bede, also placed the building of the Wall at the very end of the Roman occupation (Winterbottom 1978: 21, 22–23, 93–94). We have no direct evidence for Offa's knowledge of Hadrian's Wall, but he owned a copy of Bede's history, and though he is unlikely to have been able to read it himself, it could have been read to him (Levison 1946: 244–46). It may also be significant that Hadrian's Wall lay in Northumbria, the only English kingdom which never acknowledged Offa's overlordship, and the Antonine Wall not far to its north. In building his Dyke, was he perhaps trying to erect a Mercian counterpart to the prestigious Roman monuments controlled by his rivals, the Northumbrian kings? Wat's Dyke, within the confines of Mercia itself, might also have inspired emulation, but its date is disputed; it has been assigned to the fifth century, but dating of the section of Gobowen seems likely to be early ninth century (Ray and Bapty 2016: 19–20; Malim and Hayes 2008: 147–79).

If the Roman past was a possible inspiration for Offa's Dyke, another might be found in Germanic tradition. The remembrance of their ancestors was of the first importance to the élites of all the early English kingdoms (Wormald 1978: 32–90; Hunter 1974: 30–35). Tales of the legendary past were circulating in eighth-century England; the Mercian ætheling St Guthlac was inspired by 'the valiant deeds of the heroes of old', and sagas were even performed in ecclesiastical refectories, much to the indignation of the Northumbrian scholar Alcuin (Colgrave 1956: 80–81; Dummler 1895: 183; Bullough 1993: 93–125). The series of royal genealogies, mostly composed in the later eighth century, are part of the same process of memory, tracing their subjects' ancestry back to the pre-migration past (Dumville 1976). Offa's own pedigree included the name of an earlier Offa who, if he was an historical person, ruled in Angeln in the late fourth century (Newton 1993: 64–71). It has been suggested that Offa of Mercia may have deliberately developed parallels between himself and his heroic namesake (Fox 1955: 289–90; Hunter 1974: 4; Yorke 2001: 16), memories of which may underlie the thirteenth-century *Lives of the Two Offas* (Chambers 1932: 217–43; Garmondsway 1968: 233–37) composed at St Albans, a house allegedly founded and endowed by the Mercian king (Whitelock 1951: 58–64; Vaughan 1958: 41–48, 189–94). Certainly, Offa of Angeln was well-known to English as well as Scandinavian legend (Garmondsway 1968: 222–237; Chambers 1912: 84–92), and the author of *Beowulf* calls him 'the best of all mankind between the two seas' (Klaeber 1950: lines 1954–62). More pertinent in the present context is his appearance in the heroic poem *Widsith*, which remembers how 'with one sword he marked the boundary with the *Myrgyngs* at *Fifeldore*; just as Offa struck it, *Engle* and *Swaefe* have henceforth held it' (*heoldon forth siþþan Engle ond Swaefe swa hit Offa geslog*) (Chambers 1932: 244; Alexander 1966: 39). The bones of the story consist of a combat between Offa and two enemy champions on an island in a river (assumed to be the Eider), Offa being armed with an ancient sword retrieved from a grave-mound. The twelfth-century Danish historian, Saxo Grammaticus, gives the sword's name as *Skrep*, meaning 'firm, unyielding', or perhaps 'scraping' (Davidson 1979: i 109, ii 69; Chambers 1912: 91), and it is of some interest that a sword belonging to Offa of Mercia was bequeathed by the *ætheling* Æthelstan, son of King Æthelred *unraed*, to his brother, the future King Edmund II Ironside (Sawyer 1968: no. 1503); perhaps this sword was thought to be the legendary *Skrep*. The boundary in question seems to have settled by combat rather than by the building of a physical landmark, but the idea of establishing a permanent frontier may have had some influence on Offa of Mercia's construction of the Dyke which bears his name. Fox indeed adapted the quotation from *Widsith* to suit the circumstances of the Dyke: *heoldon forth siþþan Engle ond Cumbra swa hit Offa geslog* (Fox 1955: xvii, 288–90).

If we accept Offa as a likely architect of the Dyke, it remains to ask why he had it built. The theory of a negotiated frontier is no longer tenable. The form of the Dyke is clearly defensive; it looks towards Wales, and forms a formidable obstacle to anyone coming from the west. David Hill, who, as we have seen, accepts only the central reaches as the Dyke proper, proposed that it was built to defend Mercian territory from hostile incursions from the Welsh kingdom of Powys. The hypothesis is a tempting one, but there are difficulties involved, not least the lack of hard evidence for relations between Mercia and Powys in the time of Offa. Most of the English sources for the eighth century emanate from Mercia's rivals, Wessex and Northumbria, and largely ignore Mercian affairs, while on the other side of the Dyke the period between 679 and 825 has been described as 'the least well understood in the whole of Welsh history' (Charles-Edwards 2001: 94). The kingdom of Powys itself is first mentioned in the *Annales Cambriae* under the year 808, and although royal genealogies, none composed earlier than the ninth century, take the line of its kings back to around 600, there is no reason to suppose that the territory over which they ruled was coterminous with the ninth-century kingdom; like many early kingdoms, Mercia included, Powys may have been formed by 'absorption of smaller original units ... into a larger over-kingdom' (Maund 2000: 32). One such unit may have been the territory of the *Wreconsaetan* (northern Shropshire), lost to the English in the mid-seventh century (Davies 1982: 99–101).

With such a dearth of material, it is difficult to discern any significant patterns, but the handful of relevant entries in the *Annales Cambriae* (which as we have seen is a South Welsh source) show Offa at war not with the rulers of Powys, but with the southern Welsh. In 760, there was a battle between British and English at Hereford, the outcome of which is not recorded; in 778 there occurred 'the devastation of the South Britons' (*Brittonum dexteralium*) by Offa' (Welsh texts distinguish North and South Wales from the position of an observer across the Irish Sea so that the North is on the left, *sinister* and the South on the right *dexter*). In 784 occurred 'the devastation of the Britons by Offa in the summertime', while a further devastation of *Rienuch* in 795 may relate to an attack on Brycheiniog (modern Brecon) (Williams ab Ithel 1860). Finally, and 'for what it is worth', Matthew Paris in the thirteenth century alludes to hostilities between Offa and a Welsh king possibly to be identified as Maredudd of Dyfed (d. 796) (Sims-Williams 1990: 53). It may have been in the course of these campaigns that the Welsh kingdom of Ergyng, or at least the part of it which lay east of the River Wye, came under Mercian control; if the Wye was, as many have supposed, the boundary between Welsh and Mercians in Offa's time (Gelling 1992: 116–17; Fox 1955: xvii), then the gap in the Dyke between Highbury in Gloucestershire and Rushock Hill in Herefordshire is less problematic, but this may not have been the case until the early ninth century (Davies 1982: 102). By the eleventh century Ergyng, anglicized as Archenfield, was certainly 'English', and attached to Herefordshire (Erskine 1986: fo. 179).

Fragmentary as it is, the evidence tends to bear out the suggestion that the southernmost portion of Offa's Dyke at least was built against the southern Welsh kingdoms of Dyfed, Brycheiniog and Glywysing. Only after Offa's death do the *Annales Cambriae* record warfare between the Mercians and the north Welsh and then with Gwynedd rather than Powys; a battle at Rhuddlan is recorded in 796 and in 798 Caradoc, king of Gwynedd was killed by the English. Powys appears only in 822, when 'the fortress (*arx*) of Deganwy was destroyed by the English [i.e. the Mercians], and they took the kingdom of Powys into their control' (Williams ab Ithel 1860). There is, however, the evidence of the enigmatic Pillar of Eliseg, erected by Cyngen king of Powys (d. 855) in honour of his great-grandfather Eliseg/Elise (Edwards 2009: 143–77), which stands at Llantysilio-yn-ial, near the ruins of Valle Crucis Abbey, which took its name from Eliseg's 'broken cross' (Hill 2000: 202–203). The inscription which it bore is now illegible, but before it faded completely a transcription was made by the seventeenth-century antiquarian, Edward Lhyud (Hill 2000: 203), the relevant section of which reads as follows:

> + Concenn son of Cattell, Cattell son of Brohcmail, Brohcmal son of Eliseg, Eliseg son of Guoillauc.

> +Concenn therefore, great-grandson of Eliseg, erected this stone for this great-grandfather Eliseg.

> + It was Eliseg who united the inheritance of Powys ... however through force
> ... from the power of the English... land with his sword by fire(?).

> (Edwards 2013: 326).

Eliseg's exploits have been dated to the late 760s or early 770s, presumably by reckoning back through generations of thirty years duration, but a rather earlier date might be deduced from the death in 808 of his grandson Cadell, Cyngen's father, recorded in the *Annales Cambriae* (Williams ab Ithel 1860; Gelling 1992: 118). The Pillar erected in Eliseg's name certainly implies extensive hostilities between the Welsh of Powys and the Mercians, perhaps in the opening years of Offa's reign, perhaps a little earlier. The Welsh are envisaged as on the offensive, which might provide the context for a military and defensive structure along the Mercian boundary with Powys; it would be unnecessary to extend this to the Dee estuary, since the Welsh of Gwynedd were hostile to those of Powys, and likely to ally (as they had done in the seventh century) with the Mercians (Davies 1982: 113).

Warfare between the Mercians and the men of Powys might provide a context for the construction of the Dyke, but it remains to ask how it was used. There is no indication that it was ever garrisoned, but the idea that it might have been patrolled was mooted by Earle as long ago as 1857. Earle indeed believed that he had found traces of such a patrol system. He began with the record in the base text ('A') of the *Anglo-Saxon Chronicle* of the death in 896 of Wulfric, described both as the king's *horsthegn* and as a *wealhgefera* (Whitelock *et al.* 1965). The word *wealhgefera* occurs nowhere else, and its meaning is obscure; the first element certainly means 'Welsh' and the second, *gefera*, has the meaning of 'companion, retainer'. Later recensions of the Chronicle emended the text to read *wealhgerefa* ('Welsh reeve'), presumably meaning 'an official in charge of the Welsh', or perhaps 'in charge of matters concerning the Welsh'. Earle, who preferred the original reading in the 'A' recension, gave Wulfric the grandiose title of 'patroller-general of the Welsh marches', seeing him as the director of 'a patrol system, with stations of guard at certain intervals' along the length of the Dyke (Earle 1857: 205–6).

The king whom Wulfric served was, of course, Alfred of Wessex, but Earle argued that his office was no innovation of the West Saxons but a continuation of Mercian practice; he pointed to the appearance of comparable officials in a diploma of the Mercian king, Burgred, dated 855, which freed an estate in Worcestershire 'from the feeding and maintenance of those men whom we call in English *wahlfæreld*, and from lodging (*fæsting*) them and lodging all mounted men of the English race and from other peoples (*ælþeodigra*) whether of noble or humble birth' (Sawyer 1968: no. 207). Like Wulfric *wealhgefera*, the *walhfæreld* was clearly a mounted man, comparable with the royal *fæstingmen* whose entitlement to hospitality is recorded in Wessex and Kent as well as Mercia (Sawyer 1968: nos 186, 278, 1271). The word *wahlfæreld* is not found elsewhere, but its literal meaning is 'Welsh (*walh*) expedition (*færeld*)', perhaps even 'Welsh military expedition', since *færeld* comes from the same root as *fyrd*, the normal term for the English army:

both are cognate with OE *faran*, 'to make a journey' as indeed is *gefera* (Barney 1985: 24). In Earle's scenario, the *walhfæreld* become 'the military company on the Welsh service' or even more grandly, 'the *corps d'armee* on the foreign border'. He also suggested that the system was operating as late as 1053, when the *Anglo-Saxon Chronicle* records the killing by the Welsh of a large number of *weardmenn* at Westbury (Whitelock *et al.* 1965). It should be noted that whereas Whitelock translated *weardmenn* as 'patrols', Michael Swanton's translation of the *Chronicle* renders it as 'guards'; the first conveys the idea of a mobile force, the other a static group, which demonstrates nicely the importance of checking the original text before coming to any conclusions (Whitelock *et al.* 1965: 128; Swanton 1996: 184). Earle went on to compare the landlocked barrier of the Dyke with the coastguard, citing the passage in *Beowulf* where the hero, landing in Hrothgar's territory, is challenged by a coast-warden, who then leads him and his companions to the king. A similar passage describing events directly contemporary with the supposed date of Offa's Dyke occurs in the *Anglo-Saxon Chronicle* for 787 (Whitelock *et al.* 1965):

> In this year King Beorhtric [of Wessex] married Offa's daughter Eadburh. And in his days there came for the first time three ships of the Northmen, and then the reeve rode to them and wished to force them to the king's residence for he did not know what they were; and they slew him.

Of course the account in the *Chronicle* is not, as it stands, contemporary, since the text was not compiled until the reign of Alfred, but it presumably draws on some earlier account; in the late tenth century Æthelweard, using a slightly different version, adds that the ships landed at Portland, in Dorset, and gives the name of the reeve, Beaduheard, who, thinking they were trading-vessels, tried to lead their crews to the king's palace at Winchester (Campbell 1962: 27).

Earle's argument is a compelling one, though it might be (indeed was) objected that whereas the *walhfæreld* of Burgred's diploma might represent 'an English patrol of the borders', they might equally well be simply 'messengers who passed between England and Wales' (Whitelock 1955: 486). Some support for the latter interpretation comes from the law-code of Ine of Wessex (c. 694), which specifies a wergeld for 'the king's Welsh horseman who can ride on his errands' (*cyninges horswealh, se þe him mæge geærendian*) (Attenborough 1922: 46–47). Earle's concept of the Dyke as a patrolled frontier was nevertheless taken up both by Noble and Hill and Worthington, and some support for the theory can be found in the place-names of the region (Hill and Worthington 2003: 40–42, 126–127). Margaret Gelling suggested that the concentration in the Welsh marches, and especially in Shropshire, of names derived from Old English *burhtun* ('settlement belonging to the *burh*') might indicate 'remnants of a system of defensive posts and army mustering-places', and that the men in charge of such mustering points might themselves be commemorated in another group of names derived from Old English *burhweard* ('guardian of the *burh*') (Gelling 1989: 145–51, 1992: 119, 121–22). One such name survives as Bollingham House in Eardisley (Herefordshire) which coincidentally possessed a 'defensible house' (*domus defensabilis*) before 1066; only two are recorded in Domesday Book, the other being at nearby Ailey (Erskine 1986: fos 184v, 187). Gelling's theory has found some support from John Blair, who, however, interprets the *burhtunas* not as independent settlements but as outposts or guardposts of a central fortified place (the *burh*), each functioning 'as the 'eyes' of its parent site, greatly extending its field of vision' (Blair 2018: 196–219, quotation on 199). Blair gives several examples of such central settlements with their outliers, which demonstrate how such a system might work.

The fact remains that while it is possible to construct a hypothetical model for the Dyke's operation, to show how it might have been is not to show how it was. The root difficulty is best illustrated by comparison with another grandiose scheme, undertaken by another English king a hundred years after the presumed construction of Offa's Dyke. Alfred, king of the West Saxons, was faced, like Offa, with incursions from abroad, this time 'the roving fleets of seaborne heathen' known to history as the Vikings (Sawyer 1968: no. 134). One of his responses was to encircle his kingdom of Wessex not with a continuous earthwork, but with a line of *burhs*, enclosed and defended fortresses, which would not only provide refuge in case of invasion, but also a platform for attack on the enemy in his own strongholds. Many of Alfred's *burhs* still stand, and though not all are now occupied, some of them subsequently developed into towns and took on urban, rather than primarily military, characteristics. But in the case of Alfred's works, the physical evidence does not stand alone. We know of his achievements not only because his biographer Asser recorded them for posterity, but also from the survival of the *Burghal Hidage*, which describes how the *burhs* were maintained and manned (Rumble 1996: 14–35). Dating from the reign of Alfred's son and successor, Edward the Elder, the *Burghal Hidage* has been described as 'the earliest administrative record of English government that survives' (Wormald 1996: 64). It lists the fortifications built by Alfred and his son, and assigns to each an assessment in hides, the unit of taxation and service employed in England from the seventh century to the eleventh (notionally the amount of land which would support a single household for a year). It goes on to provide the basis for calculating the service due:

> For the establishment of a wall of one acre's breadth and for its defence, 16 hides are required. If each hide is represented by one man, then each pole can be furnished with four men. Then for the establishment of a wall of twenty poles, there is required eighty hides; and for a furlong, 150 hides and ten hides are required.[2]

It has to be said that this represents an ideal scenario, and that the figures given in the document frequently do not agree with the wall-lengths which can be identified today, whether still standing or recoverable by archaeological means. Nevertheless, as a

---

[2]   A pole (OE *gyrd*) was equivalent to 5½ modern yards; four poles made up an acre's breadth (22 modern yards). Ten 'broad acres' made up a furlong (220 modern yards).

statement of the method used to put into effect King Alfred's commands to build *burhs*, the *Burghal Hidage* is a remarkable text, which provides an insight into the administrative realities of its day.

It will immediately be obvious that some similar method might have been employed to construct Offa's Dyke (Hill and Worthington 2003: 116–18). Mercia was hidated in Offa's day (and indeed before), and the hidage was used to calculate obligations to service; one of Offa's own diplomas lists the food-rent (OE *feorm*) due from an estate assessed at 60 hides (Sawyer 1968: no. 146). It is also from the late eighth century that the obligation to build fortifications, along with service in the royal host, was imposed on Mercia and the other regions under Offa's control (Brooks 1971: 69–84). The weasel words, as usual, are 'might have been'; there is no indication of any Mercian predecessor to the *Burghal Hidage*. This brings us back to the heart of the problem. Alfred's court produced a biography of the king, a series of translations (some by the king himself) of works 'most needful for men to know', and the base text of the *Anglo-Saxon Chronicle*, which continued into the reign of his son Edward, when the *Burghal Hidage* also took shape. Offa's entourage produced nothing comparable that has survived. There was no Mercian chronicler, no royal biographer, no written documents except the royal diplomas, themselves preserved only sporadically, and largely in religious communities removed from the main centres of royal power; most come from the archive of Worcester Cathedral Priory and relate to the subkingdom of the *Hwicce* (roughly the modern shires of Worcester and Gloucester and south-west Warwickshire). Why this should have been so is an enigma, but the fact remains that much of what Offa did, and still more how and why he did it, is irrevocably lost to us; and this includes the genesis and nature of the Dyke which bears his name.

It may be, of course, that we are asking the wrong questions. Perhaps, instead of seeking contexts in the political and military history of the eighth century, we should see Offa's Dyke and similar structures as objects in the landscape, affecting and affected by their physical environment. Julie Wileman has set out the advantages of this approach: 'lacking good dates, and therefore historical confirmation of the intentions of the builders, we may at least be able to identify what forms of interfaces these works do not represent' (Wileman 2003: 64). In this respect, Offa's Dyke, with 'unsecured terminals' and no discernible infrastructure in the shape of 'forward defences, or accommodation for troops and supplies, or good lines of communication' looks rather ineffective for any military purpose. Its function may have been ideological, in Wileman's phrase, a 'statement in the landscape'. Paolo Squatriti, who has urged a similar approach to that of Wileman, sees the Dyke as (in part at least) a proclamation that 'the architect … was a hero rather like a Beowulf or a Hrothgar' (Squatriti 2004: 9–36). Or perhaps Offa's Dyke failed of its purpose, or at least outlived it. There is no indication of any attempt to maintain it, which is hardly surprising, given that Mercian power diminished sharply after Offa's death, to be replaced in the later ninth century by the rising star of Wessex. Nor did the Dyke play any discernible role in subsequent warfare along the English/Welsh border; in 893, for instance, an English host besieged a Viking army at Buttington (Montgomeryshire), right on the line of the Dyke, but though the river (the Severn) is mentioned as separating the combatants, the Dyke is not (Whitelock *et al.* 1965). English pressure on the Welsh kingdoms, north and south, during the later ninth century, brought the frontier west of the Dyke, and perhaps thus rendered it irrelevant, especially in the north. By the time that Edward the Elder established a burh at *Cledemutha* (Rhuddlan, Denbighshire), much of north-east Wales was under English control, if not permanently in English hands (Whitelock *et al.* 1965: annal 921).

As its original functions were forgotten or became irrelevant, the Dyke may have acquired others, not intended by its builder. Wileman, in the passage already cited above, lists the ways in which such a structure could have influenced its immediate locality, in 'forms of tenure and inheritance, subsistence strategies, language and social practices' among the communities on either side. It is, for instance, an as yet unexplained phenomenon that Wat's Dyke divides the eastern part of Flintshire, which was assessed in hides on the English pattern, from the western part, which was not; it also marks the boundary between English and Welsh place-names (Harris and Thacker 1987: 248). Not all such divisions were necessarily permanent. Offa's Dyke has been described as a barrier 'slicing through the symbiotic ties between lowland [English] and upland [Welsh] economies', but the cutting of so many gaps in its length suggests that local economic ties proved more resilient than temporary political estrangement (Squatriti 2004: 9–36).

The attempt to give Offa's Dyke a context in political and administrative history is perhaps misconceived. But it is in the nature of historians to speculate, even or perhaps especially when hard evidence is lacking. 'There is indeed a charm in the very mystery of our Grimsdykes and Wansdykes; and, as the antiquarian is half a poet, these monuments of the unknown have a power over him, and while tracing their course he seems treading the land of faëry'. The words are those of John Earle (Earle 1857: 196), and they serve to remind us that much of what has been written about the genesis, authorship, purpose and use of Offa's Dyke is little more than guesswork; informed guesswork, plausible guesswork, even likely guesswork, but guesswork all the same. In the absence of hard evidence, it is difficult to avoid the conclusion that Offa's Dyke, like so many monuments of the ancient world, is passing beyond the reach of history and becoming 'the stuff that dreams are made of'.

Acknowledgements

Thanks are due to Val Fallan, Michael Hare, and Rob Liddiard for their help in the preparation of the original article (Williams 2009), and to Howard Williams and Liam Delaney for their kindness and diligence in overseeing the revised version, whose shortcomings, of course, are entirely my own responsibility. Sincere thanks to Natalie Fryde for her support for the republication of the 2009 publication she co-edited. Further thanks to Liam Delaney for preparing Figure 1 and Julian Ravest for supplying and permitting the use of his drone photographs of Offa's Dyke (Figures 2, 3 and 5). Clwyd-Powys Archaeological Trust generously granted permission for the reproduction of Figure 4 and thanks to Gary Duckers of CPAT for help and guidance in facilitating this.

Bibliography

Manuscript sources

Alexander, M. 1966. *The Earliest English Poems.* Harmondsworth: Penguin Books.

Arnold, T. 1882. *Symeonis Monachi Opera Omnia*, ii. London: Rolls Series.

Attenborough, F.I. 1922. *The Laws of the Earliest English Kings.* Cambridge: Cambridge University Press.

Campbell, A. 1962. *The Chronicle of Æthelweard.* London: Nelson's Medieval Texts.

Colgrave, B. 1940. *Two Lives of St Cuthbert.* Cambridge: Cambridge University Press.

Colgrave, B. 1956. *Felix's Life of Guthlac.* Cambridge: Cambridge University Press.

Colgrave, B. and Mynors, R.A.B. 1969. *Bede's Ecclesiastical History of the English People* i. Oxford: Oxford Medieval Texts.

Davidson, H.E. 1979. *Saxo Grammaticus: History of the Danes.* 2 vols. Cambridge: Cambridge University Press.

Dickinson, J. 1963. *The Statesman's Book of John of Salisbury.* New York: A.A. Knopf.

Dimock J.F. 1868. *Giraldi Cambrensis Opera vi: Itinerarium Kambriae et Descriptio Kambriae.* London: Rolls Series.

Dummler, E. 1895. *Alcuini Epistolae.* Monumenta Germanica Historica, Epistolae Aevi Carolini 2.

Edwards, N. 2013. *A Corpus of Early Medieval Inscribed Stones and Stone Sculpture in Wales, Volume III: North Wales.* Cardiff: University of Wales Press.

Erskine, R.W.H. 1986. *Great Domesday. A Facsimile.* London: Alecto Historical Editions. [Cited by folio].

Finberg, H.P.R. 1961. *The Early Charters of the West Midlands.* Leicester: Leicester University Press.

Garmondsway, G. 1968. *Beowulf and its Analogues.* London: Everyman.

Hunter, J. 1912. *The Great Roll of the Pipe for the Thirtieth Year of King Henry II, AD 1183-4.* London: Pipe Roll Society 33.

James, M.R., Lloyd, J.E., and Hartland, E.S. 1923. *Walter Map's De Nugis Curialium.* Cymmrodorion Record Series 9.

Jones, T. 1952. *Brut y Tywysogyon or the Chronicle of the Princes. Peniarth MS 20 Version.* Cardiff: University of Wales Press.

Jones, T. 1971. *Brehinned y Saesson or The Kings of the Saxons.* Cardiff: University of Wales Press.

Keynes, S. and Lapidge, M. 1983. *Alfred the Great: Asser's Life of King Alfred and other contemporary sources.* Harmondsworth: Penguin Books.

Klaeber, F. 1950. *Beowulf and the Fight at Finnsburg.* 3rd edn. Boston (Mass): Boston University Press. [Cited by line].

Mynors, R.A.B. Thomson, R.M. and Winterbottom, M. 1998. *William of Malmesbury Gesta Regum Anglorum* i. Oxford: Clarendon Press.

Robertson, A.J. 1956. *Anglo-Saxon Charters.* 2nd edn. Cambridge: CUP.

Rumble, A.R. 1996. An edition and translation of the Burghal Hidage, together with Recension C of the Tribal Hidage, in D. Hill and A.R. Rumble (eds) *The Defence of Wessex: the Burghal Hidage and Anglo-Saxon Fortifications.* Manchester: Manchester University Press, 14–35.

Sawyer, P.H. 1968. *Anglo-Saxon Charters: An Annotated List and Bibliography.* London: Royal Historical Society. Revised edition, viewed 1 March 2019, http://www.esawyer.org.uk/about/index.html

Swanton, M. 1996. *The Anglo-Saxon Chronicle.* London: Dent.

Thorpe, L. 1978. *Gerald of Wales, The Journey through Wales and The Description of Wales.* Harmondsworth: Penguin Books.

Webb, C.C.I. 1909. *Ioannis Saresberiensis episcopi Carnotensis Policratici sive De Nugis Curialium* ii. Oxford: Clarendon Press.

Whitelock, D. 1955. *English Historical Documents, volume 1: c. 500–1042.* 1st edn. London: Eyre and Spottiswood.

Whitelock, D., Douglas, D.C. and Tucker, S.I. 1965. *The Anglo-Saxon Chronicle. A Revised Translation.* London: Eyre and Spottiswood. [Cited by annal].

Williams Ab Ithel, J. 1860. *Annales Cambriae.* London: Rolls series. [Cited by annal].

Winterbottom, M, 1978. *Gildas: The Ruin of Britain and other works.* Chichester: Phillimore.

Published sources

Barney, S. A. 1985. *Word-hoard. An Introduction to Old English Vocabulary.* 2nd edn. New Haven and London: Yale University Press.

Bapty, I. 2004. The final word on Offa's Dyke? Clwyd-Powys Archaeological Trust website www.cpat.org.uk/offa/offrev.htm (accessed March 29 2019).

Belford, P. 2017. Offa's Dyke: a line in the landscape, in T. Jenkins and R. Abbiss (eds), Fortress Salopia, 60–81, Solihull: Helion.

Blair, J. 2005. *The Church in Anglo-Saxon Society.* Oxford: Oxford University Press.

Blair, J. 2018. *Building Anglo-Saxon England.* Princeton and Woodstock: Princeton University Press.

Brooks, N. 1971. The development of military obligations in eighth- and ninth-century England, in P. Clemoes and K. Hughes (eds) *England before the Conquest. Studies in Primary Sources presented to Dorothy Whitelock*. Cambridge: Cambridge University Press: 69–84.

Brown, M.P. and Farr, C.A. (eds) 2001. *Mercia: an Anglo-Saxon Kingdom in Europe*. Leicester: Leicester University Press.

Bullough, D. 1993. What has Ingeld to do with Lindisfarne? *Anglo-Saxon England* 22: 93–125.

Chadwick, H.M. 1926. *The Heroic Age*. Cambridge: Cambridge University Press.

Chambers, R.W. 1912. *Widsith: a Study in Old English Heroic Legend*. Cambridge: Cambridge University Press.

Chambers, R.W. 1932. *Beowulf: an Introduction to the Study of the Poem with a discussion of the Stories of Offa and Finn*. 2nd edn. Cambridge: Cambridge University Press

Charles-Edwards, T.A.M. 2001. Wales and Mercia, in Brown and Farr 2001: 89–105.

Davies, W. 1982. *Wales in the Early Middle Ages*. Leicester: Leicester University Press.

Dumville, D.N. 1976. The Anglian collection of royal genealogies and regnal lists. *Anglo-Saxon England* 5: 22–50.

Dumville, D.N. 1977/8. Review of Hughes 1973. *Studia Celtica* 12/13: 461–67.

Earle, J. 1857. Offa's Dyke in the neighbourhood of Knighton. *Archaeologia Cambrensis* 3rd ser. 3: 196–209.

Edwards, N. 2009. Re-thinking the Pillar of Eliseg. *Antiquaries Journal* 89: 143–77.

Eyton, R.W. 1860. *Antiquities of Shropshire*, xi. London: John Russel Smith.

Fox, C. 1955. *Offa's Dyke: a Field Survey of the Western Frontier Works of Mercia in the Seventh and Eighth centuries AD*. London: The British Academy.

Fryde, N and Reitz, D. (eds) 2009. *Walls, Ramparts and Lines of Demarcation: Selected Studies from Antiquity to Modern Times*. Berlin: LIT Verlag.

Gelling, M. 1989. The place-names Burton and variants, in S.C. Hawkes (ed.) *Weapons and Warfare in Anglo-Saxon England*. Oxford: OUP: 145–53.

Gelling, M. 1992. *The West Midlands in the Early Middle Ages*. Leicester: Leicester University Press.

Hare, M. 2004. Review of Hill and Worthington 2003. *Transactions of the Bristol and Gloucestershire Archaeological Society* 122: 205–6.

Harris, B.E, and Thacker, A.T. 1987. *The Victoria History of the County of Cheshire* i. Oxford: Oxford University Press.

Hill, D. 2000. Offa's Dyke, pattern and purpose. *Antiquaries Journal* 80: 195–206.

Hill, D. and Worthington, M. 2003. *Offa's Dyke: History and Guide*. Stroud: Tempus.

Hughes, K. 1973. The Welsh Latin Chronicles: Annales Cambriae and related texts. *Proceedings of the British Academy* 59: 233–58; reprinted Hughes, K. 1980. *Celtic Britain in the Early Middle Ages.* Woodbridge: Boydell Press: 67–85.

Hunter, M. 1974. Germanic and Roman antiquity and the sense of the past in Anglo-Saxon England. *Anglo-Saxon England* 3: 29–50.

Lapidge, M. 1982. Byrhtferth and the early sections of the Historia Regum attributed to Symeon of Durham. *Anglo-Saxon England* 10: 97–122.

Levison, W. 1946. *England and the Continent in the Eighth Century.* Oxford: Oxford University Press.

Malim, T. and Hayes, L. 2008. The date and nature of Wat's Dyke: a reassessment in the light of recent investigations at Gobowen, Shropshire, in S. Crawford and H. Hamerow (eds) *Anglo-Saxon Studies in Archaeology and History 15.* Oxford: Oxbow: 147–179.

Maund, K. 2000. *The Welsh Kings: the Early Rulers of Wales.* Stroud: Tempus.

Molyneaux, G. 2012. The *Ordinance concerning the Dunsaete* and the Anglo-Welsh frontier in the late tenth and eleventh centuries. *Anglo-Saxon England* 40: 249–72.

Nelson, J. 2001. Carolingian contacts, in Brown and Farr 2001: 126–43.

Newton, S. 1993. *The Origins of Beowulf and the Pre-Viking kingdom of East Anglia.* Cambridge: Cambridge University Press.

Noble, F. 1978. Offa's Dyke Reviewed. M.Phil dissertation, Open University. Microfilm version, Offa's Dyke Association, Knighton, Powys.

Noble, F. 1983. *Offa's Dyke Reviewed.* British Archaeological Reports British Series, 114.

Nurse, K. 2001. A famous thing ... that reacheth farre in length. *New Welsh Review* 52: 21–27, viewed 1 March 2019, www.wansdyke21.org.uk/wansdyke/wanart/nurse1.htm

Nurse, K. n.d. Wat's in a name? viewed 1 March 2019, www.wansdyke21.org.uk/wansdyke/wanart/nurse2.htm

Ray, K. and Bapty, I. 2016. *Offa's Dyke: Landscape and Hegemony in Eighth-Century Britain.* Oxford: Windgather Press.

Sims-Williams, P. 1990. *Religion and Literature in Western England, 600-800.* Cambridge: Cambridge University Press.

Squatriti, P. 2004. Offa's Dyke between nature and culture. *Environmental History* 9: 9–36.

Stenton, F.M. 1971. *Anglo-Saxon England.* 3rd edn. Oxford: Oxford University Press.

Vaughan, R. 1958. *Matthew Paris.* Cambridge: Cambridge University Press.

Whitelock, D. 1951. *The Audience of Beowulf.* Oxford: Oxford University Press.

Wileman, J. 2003. The purpose of the Dykes: understanding the linear earthworks of early medieval Britain. *Landscapes* 2: 59–66.

Williams, A. 2009. Offa's Dyke: a monument without a history, in Fryde and Reitz 2000: 31–56.

Wormald, P. 1978. Bede, 'Beowulf' and the conversion of the Anglo-Saxon aristocracy, in R.T. Farrell (ed). *Bede and Anglo-Saxon England*. British Archaeological Reports British series 46: 32–90.

Wormald, P. 1996. BL Cotton MS. Otho B. xi: a supplementary note, in D. Hill and A.R. Rumble (eds). *The Defence of Wessex: the Burghal Hidage and Anglo-Saxon Fortifications*. Manchester: Manchester University Press: 59–68.

Wormald, P. 1999. *The Making of English Law from Alfred to Henry I*. Oxford: Oxford University Press.

Yorke, B. 2001. The origins of Mercia, in Brown and Farr 2001: 13–22.

Ann Williams

Email: eawilliams13@tiscali.co.uk

Wat's Dyke: An Archaeological and Historical Enigma

Margaret Worthington Hill

One of the very few published articles dedicated to the investigation of Wat's Dyke, Margaret Worthington Hill's article stemming from her University of Manchester M.Phil thesis was originally published in a special issue of the Bulletin of the John Rylands Library *published by Manchester University Press. Guest-edited by Gale R. Owen-Crocker, the theme was* Anglo-Saxon Texts and Contexts *(Worthington 1997). Her article is reprinted here with the permission of the author and with the support and permission of the guest-editor, the current editors of that journal, and Manchester University Press. This version has been revised for style (including the removal of footnote citations and the inclusion of a Bibliography) and includes new photographs taken by this journal's editors to illustrate the character of the monument at key locations mentioned in the text. The article remains an invaluable resource for those studying Wat's Dyke and it might be profitably read in conjunction with the published fieldwork and dating of Wat's Dyke at Gobowen (Shropshire) by Malim and Hayes (2008). Margaret spoke eloquently about her long-term research on Offa's Dyke and Wat's Dyke at the first meeting of the Offa's Dyke Collaboratory in Shrewsbury in April 2017 and attended the Offa's Dyke Conference at Oswestry in September 2018. In this context, it is a particular privilege to include her important study in the first volume of the* Offa's Dyke Journal, *thus recognizing her longstanding contribution to the study of Britain's longest early medieval linear earthworks.*

Keywords: linear earthwork, Wat's Dyke, Offa's Dyke Project

Wat's Dyke is a linear earthwork consisting of a bank of earth and a single ditch, a form of construction known from when people first became settled farmers with a need to enclose and defend their land and continuing into modern times (Figure 1). With such a long history of construction there are many linear earthworks in the landscape, some a few hundred metres long and some many kilometres. Their uses are as varied as their dates and sizes, but most mark a boundary the purpose of which is still clear today, for example the Bronze Age boundaries on Dartmoor separating the upland open grazing from the more intensively farmed land lower down or the earthworks which form a defensive structure across a routeway. Some are defences near the boundary of a territory; the Roman-built Antonine Wall and the Anglo-Saxon-built Offa's Dyke both fall into this category. It would seem that Wat's Dyke is also a defence along a territorial boundary, although here there is no clear historical context from which we can date its construction. Many linear earthworks are without an historical context and it is usual to turn to archaeology to provide answers to questions of 'Where is it?' 'When was it built?' and 'What was its purpose?'[1]

In general terms it is possible to provide answers to these questions for Wat's Dyke. It appears on Ordnance Survey maps and it was the subject of a report by Sir Cyril Fox in 1934 (Fox

Offa's Dyke Journal volume 1 2019
Manuscript received: 24 October 2018
accepted: 5 January 2019

Figure 1: Looking south along the bank and ditch of Wat's Dyke to the east of Ruabon. Here, the linear earthwork runs through farmland to the south of Pentre-clawdd Farm and to the north of Wynnstay Park and the A539 (Photograph: Howard Williams, 2015)

1934, 1955). The received view is that it is situated in the northern Welsh Marches running between the Dee Estuary in the north and somewhere south of Oswestry in the south but the exact line and its termination to north and south were not adequately resolved. As to when it was built, with no historical context it has traditionally been dated by comparison with Offa's Dyke because it is of similar size and construction. Wat's Dyke runs parallel to Offa's Dyke in the northern Marches, so, by analogy, it is believed to date from sometime between the seventh to the ninth centuries. The purpose of building such an earthwork would seem certainly to be as a boundary between two blocks of land and probably between two groups of people. In this case, if the dating is correct, it would have divided the Anglo-Saxon kingdom of Mercia and the Celtic west. There has however been some debate as to whether either of these two great earthworks was intended to be defensive. Fox stated that Wat's Dyke was not continuous but had been built only where natural features such as rivers and marshes would not serve the same purpose; that the exact southern termination was not clear; that its date was early medieval and probably pre-Offan and its purpose was as a boundary although the engineer had had some thought for defence in its siting. These conclusions were based on a surface examination of the remains of the Dyke, an examination which, by reference to Fox's field notebooks, can be shown to have been but a cursory examination in some of the areas where Fox had most doubt about its existence (Worthington 1986). The fieldwork described below shows many of his conclusions to have been inaccurate. However Fox's description remains a valuable record of the state of both

Offa's Dyke and Wat's Dyke in the early years of the twentieth century.

In the early 1970s it was clear that many sections of the earthwork which had been in good condition and clearly visible on the ground when Fox had described them were no longer standing. They had fallen victim to modern development as the urban areas extended along and across it, new roads and services cut through it and modern farming methods were having a detrimental effect in some areas. Clearly there was a need for new work to record the evidence before it was destroyed and to try to identify whether lengths had been lost in the more distant past in places along the line where had Fox declared that it had never been built. A programme of research, which came to be known as the Offa's Dyke Project, was begun in 1971 to investigate both Wat's Dyke and Offa's Dyke and will continue for some years to come.[2]

A search of early reports and maps reveals that although Offa's Dyke is frequently described or depicted, Wat's Dyke is not usually mentioned.[3] However many representations of Offa's Dyke in the north follow the line of Wat's Dyke. The earliest known written reference to make this mistake, if it was a mistake, is Ranulf Higden's fourteenth-century *Polychronicon*, which includes a 'Description of Britain' in which Offa's Dyke is said to reach the sea between Coleshill and the monastery of Basingwerk (Collins 1988: 24–27, 49–50). None of Higden's acknowledged sources mentions either of the Dykes and it may be that he was working from first-hand knowledge of what was currently believed as he was writing at Chester, only a short distance from Basingwerk. When his 'Description of Britain' was translated into English from the original Latin and printed by Caxton in the fifteenth century it became readily available information which seems to have been taken up by many later writers and map makers. As early as 1676 the map of Flintshire by John Speed shows a highly stylized and inaccurate line for an earthwork which is named as Offa's Dyke but which reaches the Dee Estuary at Basingwerk, the accepted northern terminus for Wat's Dyke (Speed 1676). Even where later maps were drawn from original surveys the cartographers still had a problem identifying which Dyke reached the Dee Estuary at Basingwerk: if they identified it as Wat's Dyke they were unable to provide a suitable alternative termination for Offa's Dyke since it was known from Asser's *Life of Alfred* that the latter should run 'from sea to sea' (Keynes and Lapidge 1983: 71). Thus a 1720 map by Williams which shows both Dykes has the northern end of Wat's Dyke approaching the sea near Flint, where no dyke has ever been found, and the standing dyke through Holywell and Basingwerk is named as Offa's Dyke.[4]

Some attempt was made by Thomas Pennant to set the record straight. His 1778 *Tour*

---

[2]   Research directed by Dr David Hill with extra-mural students from the University of Manchester and in recent years co-directed by the present author.

[3]   For a more detailed discussion of the maps and descriptions see Worthington (1993).

[4]   Titled: 'A New Map of the counties of Denbigh and Flint' by Will. Williams, now John Felton. L. Senex Sculpt. Printed coloured and sold by present proprietor John Felton of Oswestry, Salop'. There is a good quality photostatic copy in Hawarden Record Office, ref PM/4/6. An original copy is in the National Library of Wales, Aberystwyth.

of Wales gives a meticulous and almost totally accurate description of the line of Wat's Dyke which he concludes by saying that he has felt it necessary to give such a long description as it is often 'confounded with Offa's ditch' which he correctly states runs along a similar line between half a mile and three miles away (Rhys 1883: 349).

Rather than trying to reconstruct a northern terminus, he notes that Offa's Dyke is 'totally lost' in the area of Mold, an observation which has now been confirmed by fieldwork. The 1795 map by John Evans seems to be in broad agreement with Pennant's description but differs in some details (Evans 1795). It is by far the earliest map to give an almost accurate line for the full length of Wat's Dyke and this also ends Offa's Dyke in the area of Mold. Thus it can be seen that there was some early confusion concerning the line of Wat's Dyke, it often being conflated with Offa's Dyke in the north although there was general agreement that an earthwork ended at Basingwerk. In the south, although there was a strong tradition that Wat's Dyke ended somewhere in the Maesbury area, its exact location was unknown. Before Fox it was always assumed that this had been a continuous earthwork originally, even if its exact line was not always known.

In the nineteenth and twentieth centuries the Ordnance Survey have produced a series of accurate maps which show extant earthworks including Wat's Dyke, but because of the destruction it is represented by a highly gapped line. These Ordnance sheets were used by Fox when he examined the remains and described them and, as a gapped line was in keeping with his view of Wat's Dyke, he accepted many of the gaps as part of the original design. It was with this background that the work began from Manchester. The approach adopted by Offa's Dyke Project is initially to establish the exact line of the earthwork in a particular location. Thus, where Wat's Dyke is upstanding in two reasonably close places with an apparent gap between them, there is first an examination of early Ordnance Survey maps at a scale of 1:2500 as these give very localized information and establish whether there was an upstanding monument when the map was surveyed and drawn. Air photographs, where they are available, are also consulted as these can show clearly long lengths of field boundaries which preserve the line of the old earthwork. Occasionally they also show a crop mark across an open field. If a length seen on air photographs does not appear on the maps then the length is walked in both directions to look for traces on the ground. These may take the form of a present day field boundary with a suspiciously deep ditch or high bank, or sometimes the remains of the bank can be seen only in a hedge which crosses the line and where the hedge has prevented ploughing from completely destroying the upstanding earthwork. If a crop mark can be seen on an air photograph then its position on the ground is identified. When a probable line has been located on the ground a geophysical survey is carried out using a resistivity meter to identify areas below the surface which are either drier or wetter than the surrounding area. Where these form a linear feature, either drier in the area of a former bank or wetter in the area of a former ditch, it is taken to be evidence for the Dyke. This is then tested by excavation, the diagnostic feature being the ditch which is larger than any normal field boundary ditch.

There have been 67 excavations on Wat's Dyke, all but nine by the Offa's Dyke Project, and the forty ditch sections have shown it to be of a regular form depending on the nature of the topography over which it is built. The bank is not available for examination as often as the ditch; it is the first thing to be destroyed, and as many excavations are in apparent gaps there is usually no bank left. Where the bank is upstanding the earthwork is usually designated a scheduled monument and so is protected by law and to seek permission to destroy it archaeologically, even in the name of research, is not reasonable. There have, however, been twenty-four occasions when it has been possible to examine the structure of what remained of the bank prior to its destruction for other reasons, new roads and buildings being the most frequent. As with the ditch, there is a consistent build to the bank which, on level ground, takes the form of a turf revetting wall to the front above the ditch and a dump bank formed from material dug from the ditch. In some cases there is a turf revetting wall to the rear. In a number of places where it has been tested along the length from the south to the steep slopes of the Dee/Ceiriog confluence, there seems to be a line of stone beneath the bank which may have been a way of marking the line the Dyke was to take prior to it being built. A shallow ditch, little more than a furrow, may have served the same marking out purpose in other areas. These marking out features only survive where they have been covered by the bank; if they were originally on the line where the ditch was dug they would disappear as it was excavated.

Having established the line taken by the Dyke the next stage is to make a comprehensive and objective record by completing a detailed measured survey. This takes the form of a full profile across the bank and ditch at every hundred metres. Readings for the top of the bank and the bottom of the ditch (as it appears today), together with one for the ground level to the west of the ditch, are taken at 25m-intervals between the profiles. In this way an accurate and objective view of the condition of Dyke today can be shown diagrammatically. As all levels taken are recorded as a height above sea level, the rise and fall of the country across which the Dyke was built can also be plotted together with the surviving height of the bank and depth of the ditch to give a longitudinal section of the monument. A detailed description of the Dyke and how it relates to the landscape is also written at every profile point. One of the great benefits of such a painstaking survey is the length of time it takes. As trained students move the survey along and take the readings, the writer is able to look about and assess the siting of the Dyke as the written description is prepared. Some lengths are visited many times at different time of year and are walked from both directions along the length and along both the western ditch side and the eastern bank side. Each visit reveals a new insight and, as only the present writer is preparing the descriptions, a direct comparison can be made between different lengths. The same approach is being adopted on Offa's Dyke and similarities and differences between the two earthworks can be noted.

So what has been learned from the extended examination of Wat's Dyke by Manchester students and by the present author in particular? The earthwork extends for over 62km from Maesbury in the south to Basingwerk in the north (Figure 2). The ditch is always

Figure 2: Looking south and uphill where Wat's Dyke descends into the Greenfield Valley south of Basingwerk Abbey, Flintshire. This is the farthest north the line of Wat's Dyke can be traced on the ground (Photograph: Howard Williams, 2019)

situated on the Welsh side of the bank. Excavation has shown that, when built on level ground, the bank averages 10m wide and the ditch averages 5m wide and 2m deep forming a barrier some 15m wide and at least 4.5m high from the bottom of the ditch to the top of the bank. Where it was built along the line of steeply sloping ground, as it is where it takes advantage of river valleys, then a different construction method was used. In these locations the natural slope of the ground is cut back to steepen it still further and the resultant earth is built into a bank downslope. In this way the earthwork appears to have a deep ditch with the minimum of effort. The steepness of the slope dictates the exact method of construction (Cookson 1979). Unfortunately this type of structure is easily eroded and is difficult to find archaeologically as so little change has been made to the natural shape of the ground surface. Fortunately the Project has excavated a sufficient number of sites to prove, beyond doubt in some areas and to provide a high degree of probability in other areas, that originally there was a continuous earthwork even along the steep valley sides where Fox, basing his opinion on surface observation alone, considered an earthwork had been unnecessary. It would seem, therefore, that the methods of construction and the siting of Wat's Dyke show that it was designed and built as a single continuous earthwork.

As noted above, the recording of a measured survey and description has given new insights into the siting of the earthwork in the landscape. The full earthwork can be considered in three major sections (Figure 3): the southern section from the area of the River Vyrnwy to the crossing of the River Ceiriog and the River Dee; the central section from the River Dee to the River Alyn and the northern section from the River Alyn to the Dee estuary at Basingwerk. In the southern section there are long lengths of upstanding earthwork, mainly on reasonably level ground, sometimes with a visible, if now silted, ditch. Excavations have shown that the earthwork was built with a full 2 m-deep ditch and we can assume a similarly substantial bank from the size of the remains today, which can be as much as one to 1.5m high. The line lies outside the original built-up area of Oswestry. Modern development has preserved its line in property boundaries although in some cases destroying the monument in the process. It approaches the Iron Age hillfort of Old Oswestry from south and north on lines which give good visibility to the west but which would not make the best use of the natural contours of the hill itself if the hillfort had not already been in existence (Figure 4). Had the hill top not had a pre-existing circuit of banks and ditches, our knowledge of the preferred siting of Wat's Dyke tells us that it would probably have swept forward and upwards taking advantage of this natural sighting place. As it is, the line holds back, leaving the already ancient earthworks to dominate the countryside to the west. The clear line, proved by survey and excavation, continues to Esgob Mill.

There are, however, two major problems in the southern section: firstly the exact location of the southern terminus and secondly whether an earthwork was originally built along the 5 km of steep valley sides which exist in the area of the confluence of the River Ceiriog and the River Dee. The early records all show the southern terminus in the Maesbury area; the modern 1:25,000 Ordnance Survey maps place it at Maesbury Road where the last upstanding length of bank and ditch is to be seen. Fox considered the terminus to be about half a kilometre to the south of this point at Pentre Coed where discontinuous fragments can be observed along the meandering Morda Brook. He had considered and then rejected a continuation along this stream to Newbridge almost 1.5km south of Pentre Coed. On the ground there is a lane which seems to continue the straight alignment of the Dyke southwards which suggested that it continued even further than Fox ever considered; perhaps another three quarters of a kilometre could be added taking it to the point where the Montgomery Canal had cut the lane and destroyed any evidence of a possible extension of the line. These additional lengths south of Pentre Coed are difficult to prove archaeologically as for most of the length there is a modern road where the bank should be and the Morda Brook runs in what would have been the ditch. The matter would probably have had to have been left unresolved but for the fortuitous discovery of a linear crop mark south of the Montgomery canal on an alignment which could reasonably be seen as a southerly continuation of Wat's Dyke (Jones 1979) (Figure 5).

Several excavations across this crop mark have proved that a full scale ditch between 1.5m and 2m deep, and by inference a bank, had once crossed the fields, although only

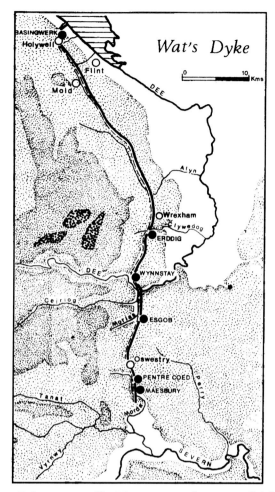

Figure 3: The line of Wat's Dyke as mapped by Margaret Worthington-Hill (after Worthington 1997).

a few lengths of modern field boundary coincide with this line. In the south the crop mark ends abruptly at a point which, on the ground, marks a slight break in slope sufficient to render the land to the south too wet to plough until recent drainage works. Since there is always a possibility that a change in geology might render the ground less susceptible to crop marks, the end of the crop mark was located on the ground and resistivity survey carried out beyond it. Although there was a clear anomaly registering across the crop mark itself, this ended at the point where the crop mark ceased to show on the air photographs. A trench was then excavated immediately south of the crop mark and, although it was extended for a considerable distance to ensure that it took in any possible change of alignment, no evidence for a ditch or any disturbance to the geology could be found. Evidence was sought for a sharper divergence from the general line. Such divergences are not found along the earthwork unless necessitated by the topography, and no evidence was found in this area. Flights over the area and field walking looked for a line further to the south and two further excavations were carried

Figure 4: Looking south along the line of Wat's Dyke towards Old Oswestry hillfort. The dyke's bank is preserved in the field boundary, the ditch is now part of the ploughed field. The shift in alignment of the Dyke can be clearly seen as it runs up to the hillfort (Photograph: Howard Williams, 2019)

out on a possible line suggested by the field boundary pattern, but all with negative results. The inescapable conclusion, on the evidence available at present, is that the earthwork finished as indicated by the crop mark. This is the last dry ground before a marshy area as the confluence of the Morda Brook and the River Vyrnwy is approached. The possibility must exist that a timber palisade was constructed as a continuation from this point although there are no known examples of such a construction on either Wat's Dyke or on Offa's Dyke. However a possible reason for a plausible terminus here is discussed below when the historical setting of the Dyke is considered.

The second problem with the southern section concerns its approach to and crossing of the River Ceiriog and the River Dee. The clear line of the Dyke finishes near Esgob Mill as the valley of the Morlas Brook is approached. The ground in the area has been seriously disturbed by the extraction of sand and gravel, possibly when the sewage works was built and by the construction of a light railway. The Ordnance Survey maps are marked with 'Wat's Dyke (remains of)' but little surface evidence remains. At two places, however, excavation has revealed the remains of a man-made bank: one excavation was on a spur of land which seems to have been at the northern limit of the modern extractive activities and the other, which also recovered a slight counterscarp bank, was to its

Figure 5: The oblique aerial photograph of a linear cropmark visible in the foreground and continuing northwards towards Maesbrook. Taken near Morton Pool, Shropshire by Chris Musson in 1984. Oswestry and Old Oswestry Hillfort are in the distance top-left (Reproduced courtesy of CPAT: Photo Number 84-c-0109)

north where the plateau met the steep valley side. There are then nearly 6 km of steep valley sides before the next excavation which proves the presence of Wat's Dyke, in Wynnstay Park. This writer has carried out extensive field work along the valley sides and considers that there is sufficient surface evidence to suggest the form of the Dyke in this section. Most of the length is made up of a plateau which gives way abruptly to the valley side: first along the Morlas Brook, then the River Ceiriog and finally the River Dee. Excavation has shown an earthwork to be present along the southern length of the Morlas Brook and similar down slope counterscarp banks can be seen in a number of places along this entire length. This is exactly the configuration that the work in the north had led us to expect. Weight is added to this identification of a built earthwork by the presence of banks running down the sides of a number of the small cross valleys which cut back into the plateau. Unfortunately the area is densely wooded and mainly used to rear pheasants all of which hinders attempts at excavation. It is hoped that a suitable opportunity will be found at a future date to test this hypothesis.

The central section from the River Dee to the River Alyn has presented a different set of problems. The earthwork is clearly visible for considerable distances and gives a very strong indication of its effective use of the topography to dominate the land to the west. It clearly follows the natural contours and so has a slightly sinuous course in places. At Wynnstay Park and at Erddig Park the line runs through country estates where there has been extensive landscaping but early maps and air photographs have established the line which has been tested by excavation (Figures 6 and 7). North of Erddig Park the line lies through the centre of Wrexham. However, it has been clearly visible into modern times and so appears on early maps and is preserved in boundaries within the built-up area. It is put to a novel use as it passes through a cemetery: here the graves are neatly aligned east/west as usual to each side of the bank but there is a series of north/south graves cut into the bank itself. The railway line has then obliterated a long length although some traces of bank can still be seen. In the northern suburbs of Wrexham, housing has encroached upon the bank but the most recent housing development has recognized its archaeological and historical importance and left a long, moderately-wide green corridor to protect it (Figure 8). Cut by the by-pass it emerges again, somewhat battered, in a solitary field before plunging through a rubbish dump and into the valley of the Alyn. Thus it is in the central section that a clear line can be followed despite substantial portions having been destroyed over the years. Excavations have shown that here, as in the area to north and south of Oswestry, a substantial barrier was formed against the western Welsh people.

From the River Alyn the northern section crosses a countryside which is deeply cut by a series of minor streams. As these run in a direction which suited the Dyke's engineer they have been incorporated into its build. Here it was first proved that the steep valley side had been scarped back and a counterscarp bank built from the spoil. Where the valley side is less steep a stronger bank was built and the remains of the earthwork in these areas are more readily visible today. More than twenty excavations have been carried out together with detailed survey and all places tested have confirmed the presence of a built Dyke. It seems certain therefore that despite the nature of the terrain there was a continuous built Dyke. As this can be proved in the north it seems likely that future work will confirm a continuous built Dyke in the valleys of the Dee and the Ceiriog.

This précis of our present knowledge of the structure and line of Wat's Dyke is drawn from many years of work which has involved many people for short times and a few for far longer periods. Without their efforts it would not have been possible to produce the excavated and surveyed evidence to prove the hypotheses formed from maps, air photographs and field walking. We have now answered the first question as to where Wat's Dyke is to be found and can turn our attention to when it was built. We have no attested historical date for Wat's Dyke, its first mention by name not occurring until the fifteenth century and so another method of dating must be sought (Palmer 1897). It has already been noted that the generally accepted date is within the early medieval period by analogy with the better attested dating of Offa's Dyke. It would therefore seem a reasonable first step to look for confirmation of this date range by an archaeological examination of the relationship between Wat's Dyke and other remains which are dated. However no Roman structure is known to coincide with Wat's Dyke and so a post-Roman date cannot be confirmed by this method. There are at least two and possibly three Iron Age hillforts on its line but the surface evidence at the two certain hillforts, Old Oswestry (Figure 4) and Llay promontory fort, do not elucidate the relationship although a strong topographical case has been made above for Wat's Dyke post-dating Old Oswestry. Even if this were taken as proof positive of a postIron Age date it does not bring us conclusively to the early medieval period. At Erddig Park, however, there are the remains of a Norman motte and bailey castle which sit atop Wat's Dyke and so gives some support to a date of construction in the Roman or early medieval period but leaves us with a thousand years in which to find an historical setting.

It might be thought that, with so many excavations, a reasonably accurate date could be ascertained based on the artefacts recovered. Unfortunately no artefact has been found in a sealed context within the bank and those found in the ditch fill have been no earlier that the seventeenth century and often more modern than this, representing the late filling in of the ditch. The lowest levels of ditch fill are barren of artefacts. The lack of artefacts would favour an early medieval date rather than a Roman one as in the early medieval period the area was aceramic and, this far west, early medieval coins have rarely been found outside towns. The excavations have also failed to find wood or bones in sealed contexts which might have given a radio-carbon date nor have they uncovered structural timbers with the potential for either a radio-carbon date or a more precise dendrochronological date. Two attempts have been made to ascertain a date, both by experimental scientific methods. The first was from an old ground surface sealed under the bank near Buckley in Clwyd. The method depended upon the orientation of particles of iron becoming fixed in their orientation as the bank consolidated. As magnetic north changes and its changes through time are known it would be possible to fix the period in which the bank had been built.

Figure 6: Wat's Dyke south of Erddig Park looking south. The bank preserved in a field boundary and the ditch survives as a shallow depression to its west: (Photograph: Howard Williams, 2019)

Figure 7: Looking south-east along the line of Wat's Dyke where it runs along the top of the south-west-facing scarp slope above the Afon Clwywedog in Erddig Park. Here the Dyke's bank and ditch are well preserved. The vegetation has been managed by National Trust volunteers. Private properties of a Wrexham suburb abut the top of the bank (Photograph: Howard Williams, 2019)

Figure 8: Wat's Dyke in the Wrexham suburbs where it now constitutes the western boundary of Wat's Dyke Primary School. Looking north in this photo, the bank is clearly preserved beneath the hedge and fence while the ditch is broad and shallow but discernible (Photograph: Howard Williams, 2019)

Unfortunately this attempt was foiled when the samples were examined in the laboratory and showed that the bank had slumped during its consolidation. A sample taken at the same time from higher in the bank material provided a sample of charcoal which could be radiocarbon dated. That this sample would date the construction of the bank depended upon the fact that adhering to the charcoal were particles of a glassy substance which was attached to particles of partially burnt sub soil. It seemed possible therefore that the burning had taken place during the excavation of the ditch through an undisturbed subsoil, although the possibility that the ditch had been dug through a previously occupied land surface had to be considered. The results of the radiocarbon dating of this sample gave it a date within the Bronze Age, a date which other considerations such as the Dyke's relationship with Old Oswestry and the Domesday evidence discussed below, makes unlikely and therefore the second possibility of how the charcoal came to rest within the bank now seems more likely.[5]

With both traditional excavation methods and experimental scientific methods of archaeology failing to date the building of Wat's Dyke, a more detailed consideration was given to the possibility of an historical context providing an answer. This was not an exhaustive documentary search but did lead to some interesting preliminary

---

[5]   This is the personal view of the present writer who was present at the excavation and taking of samples by the late, Dr A.J. Clark.

results. The earliest detailed documentary source which we have which might have a relevance to the monument is Domesday Book,[6] containing as it does information for both 1086 when the survey was taken and also the pre-1066 situation where this could be ascertained. This document would post-date the building of the monument if the proposed early medieval date is correct. A note in the Shropshire Domesday draws attention to the relationship of the Domesday boundary to Offa's Dyke and it is further noted that settlements which were hidated were 'therefore of long-standing English settlement'. The hidation of the land is simply a basis for calculating the tax due from the manor, in much the same way as the recent rateable values of properties, so that at any time a statement could be made that gave the amount of coin or service that was due from each hide. If we are looking for an early boundary between Mercia and Wales, therefore, we should consider the position of the hidated lands as the Welsh system of taxation was based on the *cantref* system of land division rather than hidated land and was still rendered in goods such as grain, cattle or honey at Domesday.

Wat's Dyke in Shropshire is in the hundred of Merset, which means the people who lived on the Mere or Mark, that is the boundary. Within the hundred the manors are listed with their hidation and it is possible to identify the most westerly manors (Figure 9). Maesbury is one of these manors and it is noted in Domesday that it was the hundred meeting place before this was moved to Oswestry. The first element in this place-name is probably the same as the hundred name rather than the Welsh *maes* meaning field. This would give a meaning of the *burh* or fortified place on the boundary.

It will be recalled from the discussion of the line of Wat's Dyke above that Maesbury is at the extreme southern end of the earthwork. When the other western manors are located it becomes clear that the boundary between the Anglo-Saxon hidated land and the early medieval Welsh land under Anglo-Norman control is not the modern boundary of Shropshire but is along the line of Wat's Dyke.

When a similar examination of the Domesday evidence is carried out in Cheshire the correlation between the limit of hidated land and Wat's Dyke continues to be remarkable, most hidated manors being to the east of the Dyke; the two exceptions are Hope (hidated) and the large manor of Bistre (unhidated) which are astride it, although not all places in this latter manor have been identified. What is more remarkable is that in the north the two hundreds of Deeside (hidated) and Tegeingal (unhidated) keep to the line of Wat's Dyke, leaving a narrow coastal strip to the AngloSaxon side as far as Fulbrook in the area of Basingwerk, the northern terminus of Wat's Dyke and, incidentally, another fortification place-name. Thus in Cheshire and in Shropshire the division between hidated land and unhidated land which is recorded as being under Anglo-Saxon control is on or adjacent to the line of Wat's Dyke.

If this examination of the Domesday evidence is extended southwards in Shropshire, beyond the southern terminus of Wat's Dyke, it can be shown that beyond Maesbury there are two manors, Maesbrook and Bausley, which are situated in line with Wat's Dyke if its course at Maesbury is projected southwards, although, as noted above, there is no archaeological evidence that this was ever the case. Beyond this is a large block of land valued at 52.5 hides which is attached to Montgomery castle. Before 1066 it was all waste but by 1086 the northern lowland part of the area was productive and included the early timber motte and bailey castle of Hen Domen, the precursor of Montgomery castle; the southern, upland, area was given over to hunting. Offa's Dyke runs through this block of land but it is the River Severn to the west which forms the boundary of the hidated land, not the earthwork. South from this block of land, however, the division between hidated and unhidated land seems to be Offa's Dyke.

The fact that Wat's Dyke marks the limit of hidated land in the north, when it might have been expected to be the more westerly Offa's Dyke, raises interesting questions concerning the relative dating of the two monuments. Were Wat's Dyke north of the River Severn and the southern part of Offa's Dyke contemporary? What then would be the status of Offa's Dyke north of the River Severn? Could there be some truth in a locally-held belief that the northern end of Wat's Dyke was called Offa's Dyke or is this simply confusion arising from the antiquarian sources discussed above? A possible northern link between the two monuments was once considered (Hill 1974) but a search for archaeological evidence between Offa's Dyke and Wat's Dyke in this area did not result in any support for the theory and so this particular idea has now been abandoned.

For the present we must consider the facts as we can discern them, that is that Wat's Dyke is a separate earthwork running between Basingwerk and the Dee estuary in the north and ending near Maesbury and the River Vyrnwy in the south. Archaeologically it has been shown to be of one build as its form responds in exactly the same way to the topography over which it is built. This line can also be shown to be the limit of hidation as identified at Domesday and the hidated land is thought to mark the extent of the longstanding Anglo-Saxon occupation, the unhidated land controlled by the Normans in 1086 representing an overlordship of Welsh lands which took place after hidation. Such a situation pertains along the full length of the Welsh Marches, however, and does not therefore offer an explanation as to why Wat's Dyke only extends for part of this distance.

If we look at the situation from the Welsh side of Wat's Dyke rather than the Anglo-Saxon or Norman side, then the hundred of Merset in the south marches with the cantref of Cynllaith, and whilst it is generally agreed that it is almost impossible to draw an accurate boundary for the Welsh principalities at any date in the early medieval period as they are subject to rapid political change, Rees's map shows the southern boundary of Cynllaith in the area of the River Vyrnwy (Rees 1959: plate 29). The River Cynllaith rises near Pen-y-gwely and is a tributary of the River Tanat which is itself a tributary of the River Vyrnwy. If Wat's Dyke was built at a time when the boundary of Cynllaith was significant, then the River Vyrnwy, or the marshy area to its north, becomes a sensible place for the terminus.

Hidated Manors
1 Bagillt
2 Coleshill
3 Radington (lost
   place near Flint)
4 Leadbrook
5 Llys Edwin
6 Soughton
7 Broughton
8 Kinnerton (?)
9 Hope
10 Gresford
11 Eyton
12 Erbistock
13 Weston Rhyn
14 Weston Coton
15 Maesbury
16 Morton
17 Maesbrook
18 Melverley
19 Bausley

Unhidated Manors
A Fulbrook
   (Greenfield)
B Gellilyfydy
C Calcot
D Brynford
E Halkyn
F Gwysaney
G Hendrebiffa
H Bryncoed
I Bistre
J Rhos Ithel

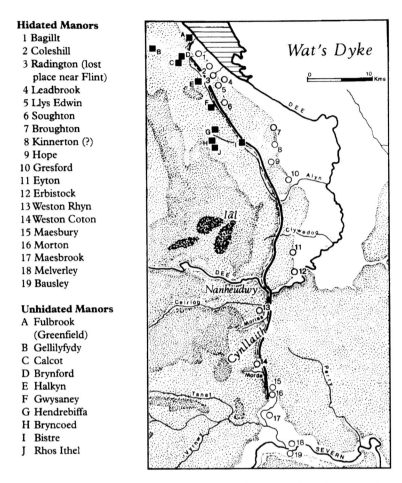

Figure 9: Hidated and unhidated manors on either side of Wat's Dyke (after Worthington 1997)

Cynllaith and, to its west, Edyrnion were unhidated areas which were held at Domesday by Reginald the sheriff who also held Oswestry Castle which controlled the route into Cynllaith from England. Iâl, also unhidated, was held by Earl Hugh from Earl Roger and although Nanheudwy is not mentioned by name, it is suggested that the entry at 4.1,13 refers to this block of land which stands adjacent to the hidated land in the central section of Wat's Dyke. In the north there are individual unhidated manors listed to the west of Wat's Dyke. It should be remembered that whereas the Anglo-Saxon kingdoms were clearly defined by the late seventh century, albeit with shifting borders and changes in dominance, the political units in Wales were smaller and still based on the kin group; thus the smallest unit would be the extended family group which belonged within a larger tribal grouping which in turn would be part of a confederacy of tribes represented by such principalities as Powys and Gwynedd. The Welsh areas mentioned above therefore represent the middle type of grouping, the tribal area which is termed in Domesday Shropshire as *finis* and an editorial note explains that whilst this usually means 'boundary, end, limit' in its singular form, here it seems to have its plural meaning of 'land' or 'territory' where the Welsh term *cantref* would seem to be needed. Perhaps we should consider whether this was a deliberate use of the word, used here to indicate not only the area of land but also its position on the boundary, as 'marches' is used in English.

Thus Wat's Dyke marks the boundary between long-standing English controlled land and recently acquired land, as indicated by whether the land was hidated or not at Domesday. It follows from this that Wat's Dyke must have been built prior to hidation as the careful siting of Wat's Dyke to control the landscape precludes it having been built along the edge of already hidated land. Thus we are led to seek a date for the building of Wat's Dyke which is before the hidation became securely settled; such a date cannot be easily resolved but recent research suggests that the date is before the reign of King Offa of Mercia (Davies and Vierck 1974; Abels 1988). Domesday offers us another opportunity to study the situation along Wat's Dyke as it also lists those manors which were waste. In the north the hidated land was productive and the unhidated land was not. However Gresford was waste. This was a very large manor of thirteen hides which seems to include Radnor and *Chespuic*. This block of waste land is between Wat's Dyke and the River Dee and must surely represent the lands mentioned in Cheshire Domesday, where, under the hundred of Maelor Cymraeg[7] it is stated that: 'King Edward gave to King Gruffydd all the land that lies beyond the river called Dee. But when King Gruffydd wronged him, he took this land from him and gave it back to the Bishop of Chester and to all his men, who had formerly held it.' (Cheshire Domesday B.7.). Thus there is almost no waste in the hidated lands along Wat's Dyke in the north, except for the anomalous area with which King Gruffydd was involved. There is no pre-1066 information for the unhidated areas of Bistre (except for one manor paying bread, butter and beer to King Gruffydd when he was in residence), Tegeingl and Rhuddlan and all the individual manors are listed as 'outliers' of these centres suggesting that we are looking at what were formerly *cantrefs* in Welsh hands. Iâl is only listed as a block of land but was waste before 1066 and it should be noted that, although listed in Shropshire Domesday, this area marches with Bistre, which is recorded in Cheshire Domesday, and Bistre was also waste and unhidated. It would seem from this evidence that, far from the Welsh raiding into England and laying it waste as is often suggested, it is only the Welsh areas which the English had laid claim to which were waste although at whose hand is unclear.

Turning to Shropshire Domesday and the southern section of Wat's Dyke we find that, as noted above, the unhidated land is not listed manor by manor, even as outliers of a centre. The Welsh lands are given their area names only. Cynllaith, Edeyrnion and Nanheudwy seem not to have been waste. The most westerly hidated manors from Weston Rhyn to Maesbury were all waste at the time of King Edward (pre-1066) but

---

[7] That is Maelor of the Welsh, compared with the area to its south and east, away from Wat's Dyke, which is Maelor Saesneg, i.e. Maelor of the Saxons.

have been brought back into cultivation by 1086. All the manors from Weston Rhyn to Bausley seem to have been in the hands of people with Anglo-Saxon names before 1066 but only Moreton and Maesbury by 1086, the remainder being held by un-named Welshmen. The presence of Welshmen is not remarkable as they occur in manors deep to the east of Wat's Dyke in Shropshire, but usually only as people present on land held by a Norman from his overlord. Here they seem to be holding the land directly from the overlord. Maesbury is a special case having been the head manor of the hundred and was held directly by King Edward, but by Domesday it was held by Reginald, who built Oswestry Castle. It was found waste but at Domesday it was back in cultivation by 'ten Welshmen with a priest', by far the highest number of Welsh recorded in a manor (Shropshire Domesday 4,1,11). So the pattern would seem to be that Weston Rhyn, Weston Coton and Maesbury, along Wat's Dyke, were waste in the time of King Edward although to the south Maesbrook, Melverley and Bausley which are beyond the southern limit of Wat's Dyke are productive and remain so throughout. Morton, which is the present day parish in which the southern terminus is situated, was in Anglo-Saxon hands, then Norman and is recorded as having suffered a short period of waste between 1066 and 1086.

It would seem that the situation along Wat's Dyke in the mid-eleventh century was one in which the Welsh side in the north was waste before and at 1066 but by 1086 had been brought back into production under Earl Hugh as far as Iâl. South of this, on the Welsh side of Wat's Dyke, we are without information for Nanheudwy but both Cynllaith and Edeyrnion seem to have been productive throughout although unhidated, whilst on the English side we have seen above that the manors along the Dyke had suffered during King Edward's reign but again were productive, though under Welshmen holding the land from Norman overlords. South of Wat's Dyke the situation seems to be the same settled conditions as those in Cynllaith and Edeyrnion. The difference between these two areas of Wales can perhaps be explained by the fact that, at Domesday, Shropshire was facing Powys, a strong kingdom at this time, whilst Cheshire was facing Gwynedd which was in the throes of civil war involving the same Gruffydd who had been in, and out of, alliance with King Edward. Thus the Domesday waste is indicative of differences along the English border which are dependent upon which Welsh kingdom they face. This evidence of the effect of the Welsh kingdoms would strengthen an argument that Wat's Dyke was built at a time when the Welsh were united between Maesbury and Basingwerk.

Thus the circumstances under which Wat's Dyke might have been built must be sought in a time which is prior to the hidation of Shropshire and Cheshire but when there is a single Welsh principality, or an alliance of Welsh princes, between Basingwerk and Maesbury. This principality would need to be unfriendly to Mercia and to hold the Dee estuary north of Basingwerk and control Cynllaith, Nanheudwy and Iâl. To account for the southern terminus, the Welsh lands to the south of Cynllaith would need to be under a different control. Thus Wat's Dyke was only necessary where the boundary between Mercia and

Wales ran with unfriendly Welsh territories. The boundary between Mercia and Powys when the latter was at its greatest extent and power and before it was joined to Gwynedd in the mid-ninth century would seem to be the best possibility, that is in the seventh and eighth centuries when Mercia had reached so far west and, in view of the hidation question, probably in the earlier part of this period rather than the later.

In conclusion, the distribution of hidated and unhidated land in Domesday Shropshire and Cheshire and the Welsh areas to the west show a close correlation with the line of Wat's Dyke. It is likely that the Dyke predated the hidation as it is carefully sited and is not an arbitrary line. That the correlation is good throughout its length suggests that it was built at a time when the conditions in Wales were the same all along its length, as the variations in the distribution of waste at Domesday clearly shows that differences could occur in England when conditions in Wales varied. Such a time of stability in Wales along the line of Wat's Dyke obtained before 850 when Powys controlled the entire area to the west of Wat's Dyke.

In the years after the Battle of Chester in 616 up to the death of Offa in 796, the kingdom of Mercia was strong and expanding its boundaries. In this period there were four powerful Mercian kings; Penda, who died in 655, is the earliest. However, Barbara Yorke (1990: 104) points out that it was only at the end of the seventh century that Mercian expansion westwards was at the expense of the kingdom of Powys and on this evidence Penda is too early. Wulfhere, a son of Penda, reigned between 658 and 675 and is recorded as being one of the most powerful kings of Mercia. Wulfhere is a possibility, but again, Yorke would see this as early for the expansion into Powys. Æthelbald, who was from a different branch of the Mercian royal family, reigned between 716 and 757, and would seem to be the most likely candidate in view of the date suggested for the Mercian expansion into Powys. He was succeeded by Offa who is himself perhaps a feasible alternative; his reign from 757 to 796 was certainly long enough to have completed two earthworks and he controlled a greatly expanded Mercia. It is however a little late to have been before the hidation of the area.

The final question asked concerned the purpose of the earthwork. It was a boundary certainly but its nature, with its substantial ditch and views to the west, is such as to make it also a defence. It must therefore have been built by the peoples to the east against those to the west. It is 62 km long and to date no evidence has been found for any structures which might have served as living quarters for a garrison and indeed such a thing would have been most unusual in Anglo-Saxon England in the seventh or eighth century. It would seem likely that it was built as a clear deterrent to raiding parties crossing from Wales into Mercia, a form of fighting much used by the western peoples who did not normally attempt long sieges or pitched battles but were extremely adept at guerrilla tactics. Such raids were endemic and as likely to take place between different sections of their own people as against outsiders; it was almost a necessity as a way for the young male to prove himself. In the case of such small raiding parties, their objectives would be to capture cattle and other easily portable objects. If the raids were more centrally controlled, however, the perpetrators may have also burned crops over wide areas making it impossible for the Mercian people living in the area to continue, thus allowing the Welsh to reclaim land which they believed to be theirs by right. Under such circumstances a dyke would act as a warning that anyone crossing it was trespassing and liable to attack. It would not have prevented a determined group crossing into Mercia but it would give the local people time to raise the hue and cry and prevent them from doing too much damage - at least in theory. We have no way of knowing what the thinking was behind the construction, how well it fulfilled its intended purpose nor how long it remained in use as a barrier. It certainly seems to have been conceived as a large solution to a large problem and we might infer that it met with some success as its line remained fossilised in the fiscal arrangements along the Marches long after it would be reasonable to assume that it had a military use.

At the beginning three questions were proposed, the where, the when and the why of Wat's Dyke. We have most certainty about the first of these as the body of detailed information collected over more than twenty years has refined its course. We can hypothesise about the when and find some support for a date in the late seventh or early eighth century in the reign of either Wulfhere or Æthelbald but there is no certainty. To some extent the question of why the earthwork was built depends on the answer to the question of when it was built, but the detailed fieldwork has been able to show its continuous nature, its uniformity of design and its strongly defensive situation. For the present the matter must rest there with the hope that one day archaeology and science will find the evidence for a firm date and once more open up the debate.

Acknowledgements

Clwyd-Powys Archaeological Trust generously granted permission for the reproduction of Figure 5. Thanks to Gary Duckers of CPAT for identifying the significance of this image in supporting the article's argument regarding the southern extent of Wat's Dyke. Special thanks to Margaret Worthington-Hill for granting permission for the re-publication of her article. Likewise, thanks to Manchester University Press, Gale Owen-Crocker and Cordelia War (the guest editor and current co-editor respectively of the *Bulletin of the John Rylands Library*) for securing permission for this article's publication in this venue.

Bibliography

Abels, R.P. 1988. *Lordship and Military Obligation in Anglo-Saxon England*. London and Berkley: University of California Press.

Collins, M. (ed.) 1988. *Caxton – The Description of Britain*. London: Sidgwick and Jackson.

Cookson, A. 1979. The Northern End of Wat's Dyke. Unpublished MA thesis, University of Manchester.

Davies, W. and Vierck, H. 1974. The contexts of tribal hidage: social aggregates and settlement patterns. *Fruhmittelalterliche Studien* 8: 224–293

Evans, J. 1795. *Maps of the six counties of North Wales*, Llwyngroes. British Library Map Library reference BM 6096 (3). Photostatic copies:John Rylands University Library reference C 155A.

Fox, C. 1934. Wat's Dyke: a field survey. *Archaeologia Cambrensis* 90: 205–278.

Fox, C. 1955. *Offa's Dyke*. London: British Academy.

Jones, G.D.B. 1979. Aerial photography in North Wales 1976–7. *Aerial Archaeology* 4: 58–64.

Hill, D. 1974. The inter-relation of Offa's and Wat's dykes. *Antiquity* 48: 309–312.

Keynes, S. and Lapidge, M. 1983. *Alfred the Great*. Harmondsworth: Penguin.

Malim, T. and Hayes, L. 2008. The date and nature of Wat's Dyke: a reassessment in the light of recent investigations at Gobowen, Shropshire. *Anglo-Saxon Studies in Archaeology and History* 15: 147–179.

Palmer, A.N. 1897. Offa's and Wat's Dykes, *Y Cymmrodor* 12: 65–86.

Rees, W. 1959. *An Historical Atlas of Wales from Early to Modern Times*. London: Faber and Faber.

Rhys, J. (ed.) 1883. *Thomas Pennant Tours in Wales*, Volume I, Caernarvon: H. Humphreys.

Speed, J. 1676. *The Theatre of Empire of Great Britain: Part 2 – Wales*. London: Bassett & Chiswell.

Worthington, M. 1986. Wat's Dyke – a comment on the work of Sir Cyril Fox in Clwyd. *Archaeology in Clwyd* 8: 14–16.

Worthington, M. 1993. Wat's Dyke – The Southern Section from the Valley of the Vyrnwy to the Valley of the Dee. Unpublished M.Phil. thesis, University of Manchester.

Worthington, M. 1997. Wat's Dyke: an archaeological and historical enigma, *Anglo-Saxon Texts and Contexts* (guest edited by G.R. Owen-Crocker). *Bulletin of the John Rylands Library* 79(3): 177–196.

Yorke, B. 1990. *Kings and Kingdoms of Early Anglo-Saxon England*. London: Seaby.

Margaret Worthington Hill

OFFA'S DYKE JOURNAL 1 2019, 80–95

Hidden Earthworks:
Excavation and Protection of Offa's and Wat's Dykes

Paul Belford

Concerns over the condition of linear earthworks in north-east Wales have resulted in a series of projects undertaken by the Clwyd-Powys Archaeological Trust (CPAT). These have taken place on both Offa's Dyke and Wat's Dyke, and on parts of those monuments that are both legally protected (scheduled) and those which have no such protection. This article reports on two such projects, jointly funded by Cadw and the National Trust, which looked at Offa's and Wat's Dykes in 2018 and 2019. Excavations took place on unscheduled sections of both monuments where little above-ground evidence survived; in both cases the work revealed well-preserved sections of ditch and bank. Samples were recovered for palaeoenvironmental analysis and dating. The implications of these results for research and protection of the monuments in the future are discussed.

Keywords: Dykes, Chirk, Erddig, excavation, scheduling

Introduction

Large sections of both Offa's Dyke and Wat's Dyke are protected as Scheduled Monuments – which is to say that they are on a list or schedule maintained on behalf of government ministers by the respective state heritage agencies; Cadw in Wales and Historic England in England. However, such scheduled sections are still vulnerable to damage; and unscheduled sections have no legal protection at all. In 2013, unauthorised damage to a scheduled section of Offa's Dyke near Chirk resulted in a programme of emergency recording undertaken by the Clwyd-Powys Archaeological Trust (CPAT) with funding from Cadw (Grant 2014). This work provided the first opportunity for radiocarbon dating on Offa's Dyke: samples of redeposited turf were taken which produced three radiocarbon dates in the period AD 430–651, together with a single later date of AD 887–1019. These dates provided a *terminus post quem* – a date after which the bank was built – although the discrepancies between the dates have not been resolved. This case was particularly prominent as it occurred at the beginning of the gestation of what became the Historic Environment (Wales) Act 2016. Questions around the protection of scheduled and unscheduled sections of linear earthwork monuments were discussed around the development of the 2016 Act, which happily was able to strengthen some of the protections for scheduled monuments (Belford 2017, 2018: 12–14).

During 2016–2017, CPAT surveyed the condition of unscheduled sections of Offa's and Wat's Dykes in Wrexham County Borough (Jones 2017). This work, which was funded by Cadw, revealed that some well-preserved and, in places, substantial lengths of both earthworks survived outside of the scheduled areas. Three separate but related strands of activity subsequently took place, informed by this work:

Offa's Dyke Journal volume 1 2019
Manuscript received: 31 July 2019
accepted: 1 September 2019

- CPAT made recommendations to Cadw for designation of those hitherto unscheduled sections of earthworks in Wrexham, in order to enhance protection of the monuments. The original scheduling process had taken place several decades previously, and changes in land use and accessibility meant that in places some well-preserved parts of both dykes were unscheduled.

- A Conservation Management Plan (CMP) for Offa's Dyke was commissioned by the Offa's Dyke Association (ODA) and funded by the ODA, Cadw and Historic England; this was undertaken by Haygarth Berry Associates and launched in 2019. Although the CMP did not include Wat's Dyke, it was an important step forward in developing a consistent approach to conserving linear earthwork monuments which could be applied to both of the monuments described in this article.

- Two excavation projects looking at unscheduled sections of both dykes were undertaken by CPAT, with funding from Cadw and the National Trust, in 2018 and 2019.

This article provides a summary overview of the third of those actions and suggests possible directions for future research and conservation. Whilst describing a specific set of circumstances – the survival, understanding and conservation of these particular monuments on National Trust properties that are also parkland landscapes – there are also broader ramifications regarding how to research and conserve Offa's and Wat's Dykes more generally, and indeed other monuments like them elsewhere in Europe.

Wat's Dyke at Erddig

Wat's Dyke is thought to have been constructed as a territorial boundary, possibly dating to the eighth or early-ninth century AD. It extended for 64km between Basingwerk (Flintshire) and Maesbury (Shropshire), and appears to have originally consisted of a rampart bank and a wide western ditch (Malim and Hayes 2008). Erddig is a stately home and estate which has been owned and managed by the National Trust since 1973. The construction of the house at Erddig began in 1684 but was not completed until the early eighteenth century. From the 1730s the estate was owned and occupied by successive generations of the Yorke family, and from 1768–1780 Philip Yorke contracted the landscape designer William Eames to create an aesthetically attractive and productive estate landscape (Oliver 2006). To do so Eames made use of some existing archaeological features, such as parts of Wat's Dyke and a motte and bailey castle, but also removed parts of Wat's Dyke near the house. Some of the upstanding remains of the dyke to the north and south of the house have been scheduled (Cadw Scheduled Monument DE152); and part of the dyke between the house and the motte and bailey was lost to a landslip in the 1980s. This exposed a section of possible bank at the north end of the scheduled area of DE152.

To the south of the house, along the west side of the drive, there is a low bank 40m long, up to 4.0m wide and 0.5m high. North of this there is no discernible bank, but instead a scarp and terrace suggesting the line of the ditch. In 1982 a section of the ditch in this area, adjacent to a cistern, was excavated under the direction of David Hill and Margaret Worthington as part of their Offa's Dyke Project (Grant and Jones 2019a: 5–6). While the results are unpublished the project archive contains a section drawing and context descriptions.

There were three aspects to the fieldwork at Erddig in 2018 (Figure 1):

- an evaluation trench across an unscheduled section of the dyke (Trench 1);
- cleaning and recording of a scheduled section exposed by recent landslip (Trench 2);
- augering to confirm the line of the dyke in front of the house.

These were undertaken by CPAT staff and volunteers with the support of National Trust staff and volunteers.

Trench 1

The evaluation trench was located approximately 40m south of the 1982 excavation at SJ 3258 4799. The line of Wat's Dyke at this point ran north–south; consequently, the trench was oriented east–west. It measured 20.0m by 1.6m in plan. Neither the bank nor ditch was evident on the surface when the trench was laid out, but substantial evidence for both emerged as the excavation proceeded (Figure 2).

The bank survived to a height of 0.7m above the original ground surface and was 9.0m wide. It had been constructed directly on undisturbed natural clay-gravel subsoil. The bank consisted of three layers. The earliest (112) comprised a dark grey gritty silt up to 0.2m thick and sealed by a thin layer of iron pan. This was overlain by an orange sandy silt (111), which was in turn capped with a clay-cobble deposit (110). Charcoal was evident within the two lower levels, and samples were taken from both of them for radiocarbon dating and Optically Stimulated Luminescence (OSL) dating. The locations of these samples are shown on Figure 3.

A shallow pit (116) was found to lie beneath the centre of the bank. This was 0.25m deep and 1.9m in diameter; it was filled with a brown silty sand which contained a single sherd of undiagnostic pottery and a small flint flake. The function of the pit is not known, but as it clearly stratigraphically pre-dated the construction of Wat's Dyke, samples were taken for radiocarbon and OSL dating.

The ditch, which had been cut through the underlying subsoil, survived to a depth of 1.5m; it was 7m wide with a small counterscarp bank (114) evident to the west which was

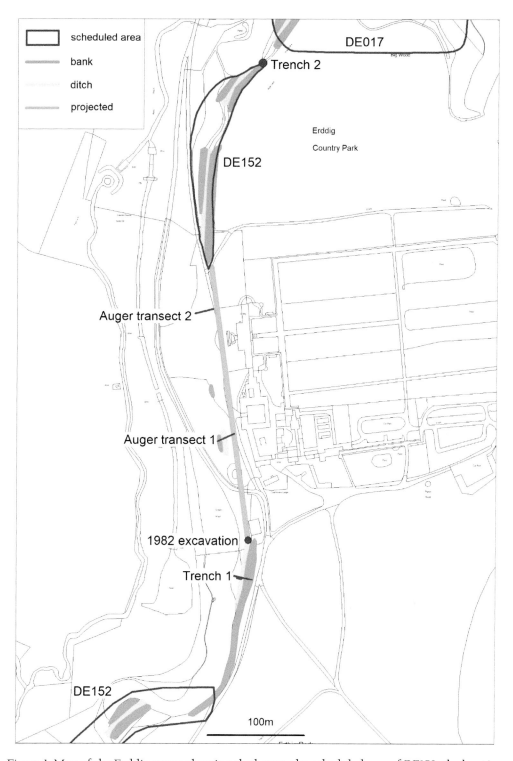

Figure 1: Map of the Erddig estate showing the house, the scheduled area of DE152, the location of the 1982 excavation, and locations of fieldwork described in the text. Original drawing by Nigel Jones © CPAT

Figure 2: Wat's Dyke at Erddig during excavation, looking east with the ditch in the foreground. The figure is kneeling at the western side of the bank. Photograph © CPAT (4526-0077)

itself 3.2m wide. The ditch had been filled by four deposits, all of which appeared to have been derived from the natural weathering of the bank. None of these contained dateable artefacts. However, the earliest ditch fill (107) contained charcoal, and again samples were taken for radiocarbon and OSL dating.

Both the bank and the ditch had been sealed by a silty clay which was similar to that found in the bank. The nature of the deposit suggested deliberate deposition rather than gradual erosion through weathering, suggesting that the upstanding bank had been levelled and used to fill the ditch. This later was in turn overlain with a silty clay containing fragments of stoneware and bottle glass consistent with a late-eighteenth or early-nineteenth century date.

Trench 2

Trench 2 investigated a section of the dyke which had been subject to a landslip, at SJ 3261 4851 (Figure 4). This revealed that the bank survived to a height of 0.8m and had been constructed directly on the original natural subsoil. As before, the extant structure of the bank consisted of three layers. Again, a putative feature was revealed beneath the centre of the bank, cut into the natural subsoil; it was 0.2m deep and 0.3m in diameter. Neither its function nor date were

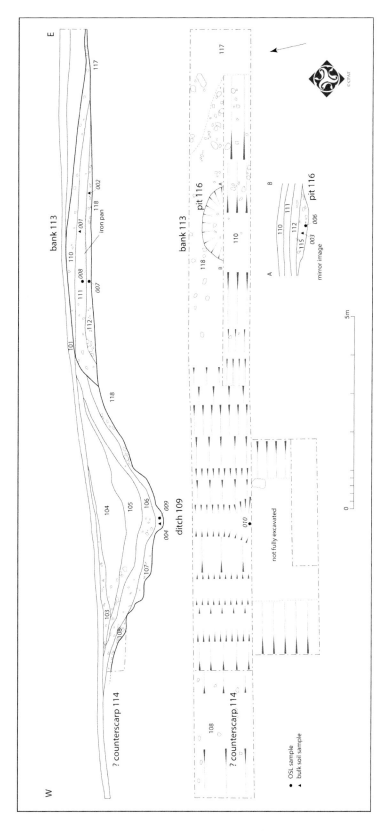

Figure 3: Plan and section of Wat's Dyke at Erddig, showing locations of samples. Original drawing by Ian Grant and Nigel Jones © CPAT

Figure 4: Cross section of Wat's Dyke at Erddig revealed in Trench 2. Photograph © CPAT (4527-0005)

evident. No material suitable for radiocarbon dating was identified in any of the recorded deposits and consequently no bulk samples were retained for further analysis.

Augering

Two auger transects were conducted across the projected line of the Dyke in front of the main house and adjoining stable block. Slight earthworks had been noted here in 2016–2017, but the extent of landscaping in the eighteenth and nineteenth centuries had been considerable. Consequently, there was no trace of the dyke on lidar at this point, even though the slight earthwork is visible to the south and north. Transect 1 consisted of seven samples over a length of 17.2m; Transect 2 consisted of six samples over a length of 17.8m. The locations of both transects are shown in Figure 1. There was a hint of the survival of a counterscarp bank in Transect 1, and the suggestion of part of the infilled ditch in Transect 2. However, in general the results were inconclusive, although it appeared that the bank had been entirely removed.

Offa's Dyke at Chirk Castle

Offa's Dyke is a linear earthwork consisting of a substantial earthen bank with a ditch to the west. Its northern section runs west of, and broadly parallel to Wat's Dyke; it typically occupies an imposing position in the landscape with commanding views westwards (Belford 2017; Ray and Bapty 2016). The known extent of 129km of earthwork makes Offa's Dyke the longest ancient monument in the United Kingdom and one of the most impressive earthworks in Europe. Traditionally associated with King Offa, who was ruler of the Saxon kingdom of Mercia between AD 757 and 796, the dyke was probably built during the hegemony of the kingdom, but its precise date, function and role have not been determined.

Chirk Castle is owned and managed by the National Trust and the line of Offa's Dyke runs through the length of the park, passing to the west of the castle. The castle was built in 1295 by Roger Mortimer de Chirk, uncle of Roger Mortimer first Earl of March. It is a stone fortress built around a rectangular courtyard with massive round towers at the corners and midway along the northern wall. The castle is situated on elevated ground on the north side of the Ceiriog valley, and commands the entrance to the valley from the west. In 1595, the castle was bought by Thomas Myddleton, and parts of it were demolished and rebuilt during and after the Civil War (Cadw/ICOMOS 1995: 39). The surrounding parkland was originally a deer park; parts of it became gradually more formalised during the seventeenth and eighteenth centuries but most of this baroque landscape was removed by extensive landscaping in the 1760s and 1770s undertaken by William Eames, on behalf of Richard Myddelton (Cadw/ICOMOS 1995: 40). These works are largely responsible for the present-day appearance of the park.

The Dyke runs through the parkland to the north-west of Chirk Castle; most of the upstanding earthwork is a scheduled monument (DE138), but at the north end part of the dyke was removed by landscaping which also created an ornamental lake which submerged a section of the dyke (Figure 5). This area was the location of excavations in 2018 and 2019.

Excavation in 2018 comprised a single trench initially measuring 29m by 1.5m and later widened on the north side for 20.0m of its length to give a full width of 3.0m (Figures 6 and 7). This trench was partly re-excavated and extended to the east in 2019, and a small trench was excavated to the south, measuring 5.0m by 2.0m (Grant and Jones 2019b). The result from both seasons of fieldwork are combined in the account which follows.

Pre-dyke activity

The remains of the bank sealed an earlier feature. This had been encountered in the 2018 excavations and part of the rationale for fieldwork in 2019 was to further elucidate its character, extent and state of preservation. It was revealed to be a large shallow pit (32), measuring at least 1.5 m in diameter and 0.4 m deep. It was filled by four successive deposits of silty clay, the earliest of which contained charcoal remains. A sample was taken from this deposit for radiocarbon dating, and from the deposit above for OSL dating.

The bank

Despite the post-medieval landscaping activities, a firm deposit of silty clay was revealed which appeared to be the very base of the former bank (24). The surviving depth of this feature was up to 0.4m deep and contained shale and cobbles, and was also characterised by mottled patches of pale grey silty clay containing iron panning, which may represent a buried turf; it extended approximately 7.0m across the trench. Beneath it, observed in a sondage, was a firm pale silty clay sealed by a thin crust of iron panning (25). It was not possible to determine whether this was another (older) layer of the bank structure, or a buried former ground surface. Charcoal was evident throughout both of these layers, and two bulk soil samples were taken to provide material suitable for radiocarbon dating.

A sequence of deposits was exposed in 2018 beyond the presumed eastern extent of the bank. This area was re-excavated and extended in 2019, partly in order to determine whether these deposits were dyke-related/to further elucidate their nature. The excavations revealed a sequence of deposits possibly associated with the construction of the bank, and with the later landscaping of the site. Elements of this included re-deposited bank material; this was sealed with a layer of silt containing coal fragments which was in turn overlain with a peaty former ground surface from which the remains of an early-twentieth-century .303 calibre rifle cartridge were recovered. It was therefore clear there had been at least two phases of re-landscaping in the general area, dating from the mid-eighteenth and early-twentieth centuries.

The ditch

The ditch (23) was at least 6m wide and up to 2.8m deep. A deposit obscured the western edge; this (34) was possibly remnant bank material or it could have been part of the fill of the underlying pit. The profile of the ditch at this point was V-shaped, with a vertically-sided trough at the bottom which was itself 0.5m wide and 1.0m deep (Figure 8). Although a V-shaped profile has been recorded in excavations elsewhere on Offa's Dyke, for example at Buttington (Hill and Worthington 2003: 65), the addition of the 'ankle breaker' has not been observed before. Generally, the profile of the ditch along the dyke has been found to be less V-shaped and more of a rounded U-shape. Indeed, Fox's excavations '400 yards north-east of [the] north boundary of Chirk Park' recorded a flat-bottomed ditch that was almost square in profile (Fox 1955: 70).

Most of the ditch fills appeared to have been derived from the weathering of the bank. The lowest (earliest) fill was a fine blue silt with iron panning and rounded cobbles; this was 0.14m deep and partly waterlogged. Above this was a 0.3m-deep silty clay, which was in turn overlain by a deep deposit (0.9m thick) of stiff blue-grey clay. Fragments of bone and an undiagnostic unglazed ceramic sherd were recovered from this latter deposit. All three lower ditch fills contained quantities of charred material likely to be suitable for radiocarbon

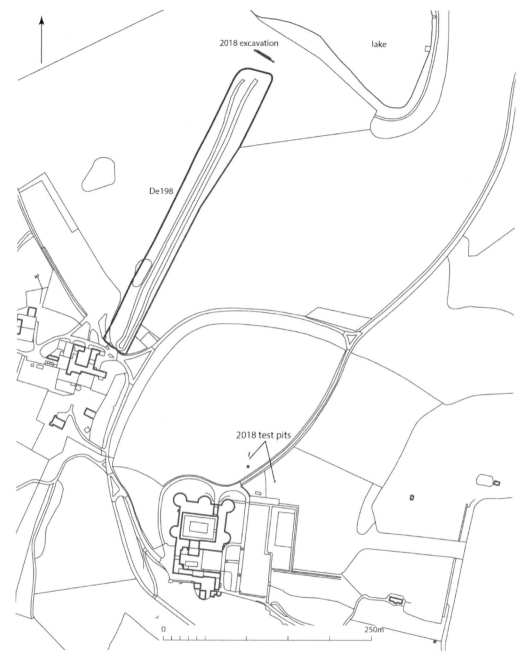

Figure 5: Map of the Chirk estate showing the castle, the lake, the scheduled area of DE198 and the locations of fieldwork described in the text. Original drawing by Nigel Jones © CPAT.

dating; consequently six bulk soil samples were taken for further scientific analysis together with two OSL cores. The locations of these samples are shown on Figure 7.

The three lower fills were sealed by a layer of orange silty clay with iron panning and following the deposition of this layer there appears to have been a long period of

Figure 6: Offa's Dyke at Chirk – a view looking south from the excavation with the scheduled part of the dyke evident beneath the trees, and the castle in the background.
Photograph © CPAT (4565-0183).

stability. The bank eroded slowly into the ditch – leaving a series of lenses of clay and shale – but there were no significant filling events until the deposition of two layers of silty clay and stone containing fragments of eighteenth and nineteenth century glass and ceramics. These clearly represented the demolition of the bank and its re-deposition filling the ditch.

There was no evidence of a counterscarp bank along the western edge of the ditch. The lidar coverage of the area suggests that there had been extensive re-landscaping of the parkland estate adjacent to and south of the lake and therefore it is likely that any remains of a bank were removed at some point in the last two hundred years.

Preservation and protection

At the time of writing the results of the programme of scientific analysis and dating are not known. However even without these results the work by CPAT at Chirk and Erddig is important for two principal reasons.

First, it highlights how both earthworks can survive in a good state of preservation below the ground, despite being virtually invisible above it. In the projects described here, both earthworks are in landscapes that were emparked in the eighteenth century

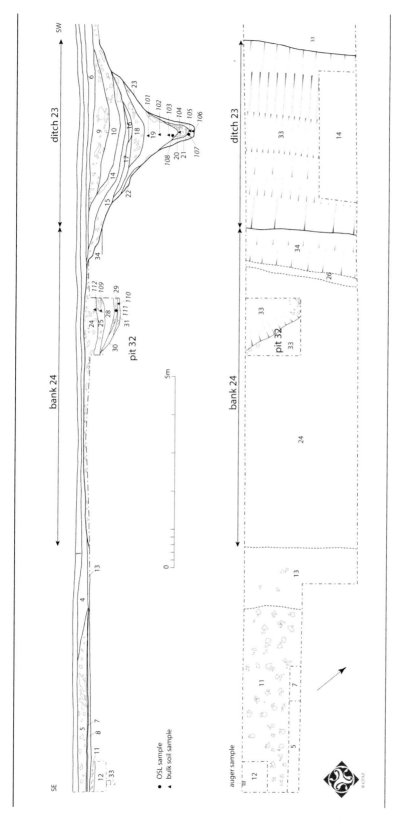

Figure 7: Plan and section of Offa's Dyke at Chirk, showing locations of samples. Original drawing by Ian Grant and Nigel Jones © CPAT

Figure 8:. The excavated section of the ditch at Chirk. Photograph © CPAT (4565-0134)

in a particular way, and this may have had a bearing on their survival. This has broader implications for the study of these and other similar monuments elsewhere. For example there is much discussion in the literature on Offa's Dyke about its original extent in Herefordshire where it is often not visible in the landscape (Fox 1955; Ray and Bapty 2016). The results from Chirk and Erddig mean that the supposed absence of both monuments must be questioned, and new research designed to investigate the possibility of below-ground survival of both banks and ditches.

Second, it shows that the advances in archaeological method and scientific techniques mean that it is possible to recover new and important information from relatively small interventions. This has implications both for research and conservation – two actions which of course go hand-in-hand (Clark 2001). However, conservation is not always as closely aligned with research as it could be. Six 'Conservation Principles' were set out by English Heritage in 2008, and subsequently restated by Historic England as the successor body for managing the historic environment in that country (English Heritage 2008). Very similar principles have also been adopted in Wales (Cadw 2011) (Table 1).

Although differently-worded and differently-ordered, both sets of principles agree that 'understanding ... significance ... is vital'. Assessment and understanding of the significance of an 'historic asset' or 'place' such as the dykes and their landscape requires consideration of four sets of values. These are: evidential value (the physical remains, including the results of previous research as well as the existing upstanding monument), historical value (the association with particular historical events or figures), aesthetic (the contribution of the 'historic asset' to the physical, cultural and social landscapes which it occupies), and communal value (the social and economic values, and spiritual meanings, that an historic asset has for the people who relate to it). There is no question that both Offa's Dyke and Wat's Dyke score highly for their significance against all four values – but it is ongoing archaeological work which contributes most to the evidential value, and indirectly to the historical value too if further dating evidence can refine understanding of the purpose for which the dykes were constructed. Therefore, it is impossible to conserve the dykes without further intrusive investigation.

Table 1: Concordance between 'Conservation Principles' issued by the state heritage agencies in England and Wales

Cadw		Historic England	
Wording	No.	*Wording*	No.
Historic assets will be managed to sustain their values	1	Significant places should be managed to sustain their values	4
Understanding the significance of historic assets is vital	2	Understanding the significance of places is vital	3
The historic environment is a shared resource	3	The historic environment is a shared resource	1
Everyone will be able to participate in sustaining the historic environment	4	Everyone should be able to participate in sustaining the historic environment	2
Decisions about change must be reasonable, transparent and consistent	5	Decisions about change must be reasonable, transparent and consistent	5
Documenting and learning from decisions is essential	6	Documenting and learning from decisions is essential	6

Issues remain with conservation of the monuments, and the risks posed to it by agricultural regimes as well as casual acts of vandalism have not gone away. Although there is a particularly fluid political situation at the time of writing, it is apparent that the coming years will bring changes to the funding arrangements for agriculture in England and Wales, and both the UK government and the Welsh government are actively engaged in consultation on these matters. An important concept that is being addressed during this consultation is the concept of 'public goods' – in other words outcomes from agricultural activities that bring wider benefits beyond productivity and economic growth. Such 'public goods' have conventionally been seen in natural environment terms, with a focus on habitat- and species-diversity, water management and quality of life. However, there is real potential for new agricultural regimes to benefit the historic environment too. This is highlighted in the Offa's Dyke Conservation Management Plan, which notes the potential scope for developing positive and active conservation of the monument through a 'mechanism for future agricultural support that ties payments to the provision of public goods' (Haygarth Berry Associates 2018: 154). One of the key findings of the Conservation Management Plan was that the greatest threat is posed by 'benign neglect', and this stems from a general lack of awareness as much as any particular land-management regime. It is worth noting that only Offa's Dyke appears to have a sufficiently high public profile to attract funding for a Conservation Management Plan – the significance of Wat's Dyke is consistently overshadowed by its more famous counterpart to the west.

Offa's Dyke and Wat's Dyke clearly have the potential to generate public interest. As noted above Offa's Dyke in particular has a high profile; damage cases such as that in 2013 generate national media attention. The Offa's Dyke Trail is a National Trail, and through it the work of the ODA in maintaining the trail is recognised both nationally and internationally. Thousands of walkers engage with the dyke in some way every year. More specifically in connection with the archaeology, over 1,000 people directly engaged with the projects described here: either through casual visits (on average 35 people a day visited the excavations at Chirk Castle) or more formal guided tours (these attracted 550 people over two days in 2018); these figures exclude the volunteers who worked on site (Grant and Jones 2019a). This is unusual, since neither Wat's nor Offa's Dyke have been integrated into heritage interpretation at either site. Indeed, many significant stretches of both dykes have public access but limited or non-existent interpretation; therefore access and visibility are combined with other challenges to awareness. Nevertheless, a latent public interest in the archaeology of the dykes can translate to a 'public good' for their conservation and management. Any conservation work dealing with the impact of vegetation, burrowing animals, livestock, pinch points or larger-scale damage should also be accompanied by considered archaeological investigation which should where possible include intrusive work to understand the stratigraphy and dating of the dykes.

Conclusion

The results of the fieldwork described in this paper provide further insights into the construction and nature of both Wat's Dyke and Offa's Dyke. They build on previous work and add further information to support subsequent field investigation. They also highlight the need for ongoing investigation in order to deliver properly informed conservation – whether on an *ad hoc* basis or as part of mechanisms for agricultural support. However future work needs to go beyond the Offa's Dyke Conservation Management Plan's recommendations for non-intrusive survey and community engagement in conservation (Haygarth Berry Associates 2018: 157). Only a comprehensive programme of archaeological excavation and public engagement will increase both understanding and awareness of both dykes to benefit their long-term survival and significance.

Acknowledgements

Fieldwork at Chirk and Erddig was funded by Cadw and the National Trust and led by Ian Grant and Nigel Jones of CPAT. Thanks are also due to Will Davies and Fiona Grant (Cadw), Kathy Laws (National Trust), Jon Hignett (National Trust Visitor Experience Manager at Chirk Castle), Jasmine Hrisca-Munn (National Trust Volunteer and Community Involvement Officer), and other CPAT and National Trust staff and volunteers.

Bibliography

Belford, P. 2017. Offa's Dyke: a line in the landscape, in T. Jenkins and R. Abbiss (eds) *Fortress Salopia*. Solihull: Helion: 60–81.

Belford, P. 2018. Politics and heritage: developments in historic environment policy and practice in Wales. *The Historic Environment: Policy and Practice* 9(2): 1–25.

Cadw 2011. Conservation Principles for the Sustainable Management of the Historic Environment in Wales. Cardiff: Cadw.

Cadw/ICOMOS 1995. Register of Landscapes, Parks and Gardens of Special Historic Interest in Wales. Part 1. Parks and Gardens: Clwyd. Cardiff: Cadw.

Clark, K. 2001. *Informed Conservation: Understanding Historic Buildings and their Landscapes for Conservation*. London: English Heritage.

English Heritage 2008. *Conservation Principles, Policies and Guidance*. London: English Heritage.

Fox, C. 1955. *Offa's Dyke*. London: British Academy.

Gallagher, C. 1996. *Chirk Castle: a Survey of the Landscape*. London: National Trust.

Grant, I. and Jones, N.W. 2019a. Wat's Dyke, Erddig, Wrexham: Community Excavation. Unpublished report. CPAT Report No. 1600.

Grant, I. 2014. Offa's Dyke DE138, Chirk, Wrexham: Survey, Excavation and recording. Unpublished report. CPAT Report No. 1224.

Grant, I. and Jones, N.W. 2019b. Chirk Castle, Wrexham: Community Excavation 2018. Unpublished report. CPAT Report No. 1631.

Haygarth Berry Associates 2018. Offa's Dyke Conservation Management Plan. Draft 30 November 2018. Offa's Dyke Association.

Hill, D. and Worthington, M. 2003. *Offa's Dyke*. Stroud: Tempus.

Jones, N.W. 2017. Offa's and Wat's Dykes in Wrexham: Monument Condition Survey. Unpublished report. CPAT Report No. 1488.

Malim, T. and Hayes, L. 2008. The date and nature of Wat's Dyke: a reassessment in the light of recent investigations at Gobowen, Shropshire, in S. Crawford and H. Hamerow (eds) *Anglo-Saxon Studies in Archaeology and History* 15. Oxford: Oxbow: 147–79.

Oliver, G. 2006. *Erddig*. National Trust Guidebook. Stroud: Tempus.

Ray, K. and Bapty, I. 2016. *Offa's Dyke. Landscape and Hegemony in Eighth-Century Britain*. Oxford: Oxbow.

Paul Belford, Director, Clwyd-Powys Archaeological Trust
Email: paul.belford@cpat.org.uk

Llywarch Hen's Dyke: Place and Narrative in Early Medieval Wales

Andy Seaman

Dykes must have been important features within the early medieval landscape, but scarcely attract more than cursory discussion in archaeological literature focused on Wales and western Britain. Analysis of a dyke recorded in a boundary clause attached to an eighth century charter in the Book of Llandaff demonstrates how a multidisciplinary approach can garner new insights into the function and significance of dykes in the early medieval landscape. Llywarch Hen's Dyke defined a large part of the bounds of Llan-gors, a royal estate in the kingdom of Brycheiniog. On the ground the dyke is represent by a prominent agricultural land boundary, but the monument also operated as a 'mnemonic peg' through which oral traditions associated with power and place were narrated.

Keywords: Book of Llandaff, Brycheiniog, charters, Llan-gors, Llywarch Hen, place-names, Wales.

Linear earthworks have rarely been afforded more than cursory discussions in the recent archaeological literature on early medieval Wales (e.g. Arnold and Davies 2000; Edwards 1997; Davies 1982). However, dykes of various forms must have been a common feature within the landscape of early medieval western Britain, which has led to their identification, analysis, and interpretation being regarded as research priorities (Edwards *et al.* 2017: 32). This article aims to demonstrate how a multidisciplinary approach can provide new insights into the function and significance of dykes in the early medieval landscape; focusing on a dyke that is recorded in the boundary clause of charter 146 in the *Book of Llandaff* (Evans and Rhys 1979: 146). This charter records the supposed donation of an estate at Llan-gors (Powys) by King Awst of Brycheiniog, and his sons, sometime in the early to mid-eighth century AD, although the boundary clause probably dates to the early eleventh century (Davies 1979: 98; Coe 2004). Llan-gors can be identified as an important royal and latterly ecclesiastical estate, associated with a monastery and unique crannog (an artificial island residence) interpreted as a seat of the Kings of Brycheiniog during the late ninth and early tenth centuries (Lane and Redknap in press). The dyke is described as *Claud Lyuarch hen* (Llywarch Hen's Dyke), a direct reference to Llywarch Hen, a legendary Brittonic ruler who features prominently in medieval Welsh poetic tradition (Sims-Williams 1993: 51-54). It is argued here that Llywarch's dyke can be identified as a *pen-clawdd* (head-dyke), an agricultural land boundary. However, whilst this earthwork offered little in terms of physical defence, the monument and the oral traditions associated are interpreted as performing a didactic role that reinforced knowledge of the boundary of the royal estate and of the status, power, and obligations of those who held it.

Offa's Dyke Journal volume 1 2019
Manuscript received: 1 March 2019
accepted: 19 August 2019

Source Material: Charter 146 in the Book of Llandaff

The Llandaff charters are the largest collection of early medieval charters from Wales, and they provide rare evidence for a period with an otherwise very ephemeral historical and archaeological record (Davies 1979). The charters are complex sources however, and it is necessary to briefly consider them before exploring the evidence from charter 146. The *Book of Llandaff* is an early twelfth-century collection of documents relating to the purported early history of the Norman See at Llandaff (Glamorgan). It includes 158 charters that claim to record grants of property made in favour of the see between the sixth and the eleventh centuries. The *Book* was compiled under the influence of Urban, the first bishop of Llandaff appointed under Norman rule, who was at the time of its compilation pursuing a series of disputes over diocesan boundaries and episcopal properties with the bishops of Hereford and St David's (Davies 2003: 17-26). The charters were compiled to support Urban's legal campaign and are demonstrably fraudulent within this twelfth-century context (Brooke 1986: 16-49). Nevertheless, Wendy Davies has demonstrated that the corpus contains a considerable number of original records, lying behind layers of later editing and interpolation (Davies 1979; Charles-Edwards 2013: 267). Thus, she argued that whilst there is no reliable evidence that Llandaff was a major ecclesiastical centre prior to the eleventh century, many of the charters were derived from genuine records that were originally compiled at, and related to, other early medieval monastic houses in south-east Wales.

The content of Charter 146 is considered in greater detail elsewhere (Seaman 2019b). Suffice to say, it contains a high proportion of interpolated twelfth-century formulae and its witness list must have been appropriated from another charter. However, when reduced to its core elements it is possible to reconstruct a record of a donation by King Awst, and his sons, of an estate at *Lann Cors*. *Lann Cors* can be confidently identified as Llan-gors (NGR: SO134276, see Figure 1) (Coe 2001: 519-20), and although the grant itself cannot be dated, Awst and his sons can be attributed orbits in the early to mid-eighth century (Davies 1979, 76; Sims-Williams 1993, 61, note 144). The boundary clauses attached to the Llandaff charters were generally not integral to the charter texts, and many are unlikely to have formed part of the original record (Davies 1979: 143). Nevertheless, Jonathon Coe's detailed analysis of their orthography has demonstrated that many of the clauses are genuine records that predate the redaction of the *Book of Llandaff* (Coe 2004), and many can be traced on the ground with a high degree of accuracy. Coe assigned the boundary clause appended to Charter 146 to his Group IV, c. 1010-1030 (Coe 2004). It should not be surprising that this date is after the likely orbit of Awst and his sons, since boundary clauses and the body of memory they preserved were contested 'living' documents, whose biographies could extend beyond their original redaction (Geary 1999: 183).

Dykes in early medieval Wales

Despite being inconspicuous in the archaeological literature, dykes must have been common features in the landscapes of early medieval Wales; such as the clusters

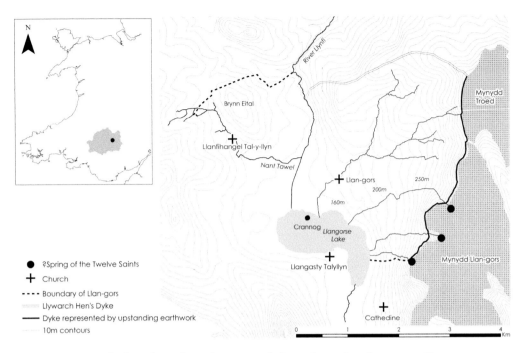

Figure 1: The kingdom of Brycheiniog and the early medieval estate at Llan-gors

of 'short dykes' in central Powys and the upland fringe of Glamorgan (see Figure 2). Around 30 of these have been positively identified, and many more are likely to either await discovery or are monuments in need of reclassification. These dykes form a heterogeneous classification of monuments; however, they are predominantly located in upland contexts occupying a range of topographic positions (Lewis 2006; RCAHMW 1976; Silvester and Hankinson 2002). Some are classified as 'cross-ridge dykes', usually with entrance gaps for trackways, whereas others cross valleys, cut across interfluvial spurs, or even cross more varied terrain. They usually consist of a single bank with or without a ditch, although bi- and multi-vallate examples are known. The banks are generally up to c. 7m wide and survive up to c. 1.5m in height, although some may have been topped with hedges or palisades. They can be up to 3km in length although most are shorter, and many are less than 100m. The Glamorgan group of dykes are poorly dated but are generally assumed to date to the early medieval period (Crampton 1966; RCAHMW 1976: Lewis 2006: 8). Indeed, a Cadw funded programme of survey and excavation on the short dykes on Powys, produced radiocarbon dates on short-life samples from buried soils that provide consistent early medieval *termini post quem* for five dykes focusing on the sixth to eighth centuries AD (Hankinson and Caseledine 2006: Table 1, 266-68). However, not all short dykes can be assumed to be early medieval constructions. The Senghenydd Dyke in Glamorgan, for example, has been identified as a later medieval deer park boundary (Lewis 2006: 58). Others may also have their origins in the prehistoric periods. Two radiocarbon dates from a buried soil below the Devil's Mouth Cross-Ridge Dyke on the eastern side of Long Mynd in Shropshire,

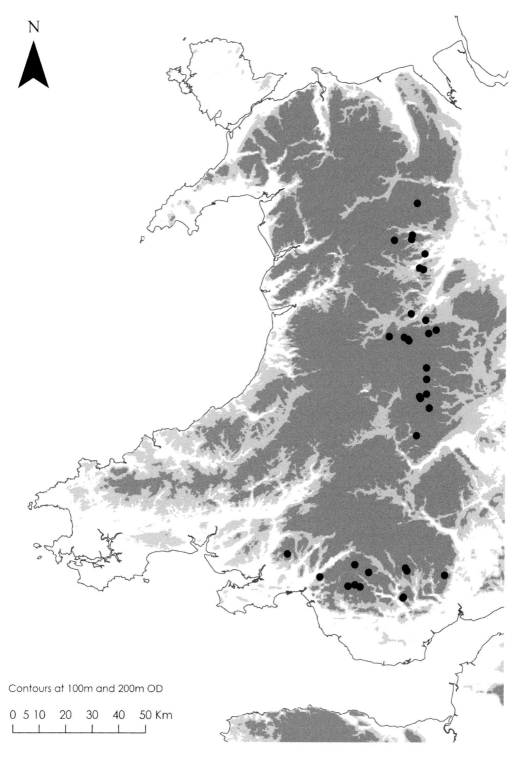

Figure 2: Short Dykes in Wales. This map is unlikely to be representative of the total distribution of these monuments. Data from: Silvester and Hankinson (2002) and Lewis (2006).

provide a Middle Bronze Age *terminus post quem* (Watson 2002: 5, 16) and is one of a number of Shropshire short dykes that are thought to be Bronze Age or early Iron Age constructions. Nevertheless, as we will see in the relation to Llywarch's dyke, we should not overlook the enduring importance of such 'ancient monuments' for early medieval communities (see also Maldonado 2015).

The Welsh short dykes were initially interpreted as defensive boundary markers, and Sir Cyril Fox saw the Powysian examples as 'evidence of the long-continued warfare between the agricultural Mercians and their 'troublesome' neighbours the Welsh highlanders' (Fox 1955: 164). However, this may not be accurate because the short dykes, as described above, have a complex and mixed provenance and appear to have been constructed by both British and Anglo-Saxon groups as well as earlier inhabitants of the landscape to serve a range of functions. Most of the cross-ridge dykes in Glamorgan, for example, are adjacent to ridgeway tracks, some of which are associated with early medieval inscribed stones (RCAHMW 1976: Figure 1). The majority of these dykes 'face' Brycheiniog to the north, but whilst some could have served a defensive function, they would have been better suited to controlling movement along droveways and transhumance tracks. In Powys, Hankinson and Caseledine (2006: 269) have noted a broad correspondence between some short dykes and the later *cantref* boundaries, suggesting that these were constructed as non-defensive territorial markers.

It should be expected for dykes to have also been common in lowland contexts and that the upland focus of many reflects survival biases. Indeed, features described as a *claud* (modern Welsh *clawdd* 'dyke' or 'ditch') appear as boundary markers in at least 22 (19%) of the 118 early medieval charter boundary clauses in the *Book of Llandaff*. Additionally, 39 (33%) of the clauses, record features described as *foss/fossa* (Latin, 'ditch'). Thus, it is somewhat surprising that monuments akin the upland short-dykes have not been recognised in lowland contexts, either as upstanding monuments or as features recorded through developer funded excavations. This must be due in part to both the comparative intensity of post-medieval agricultural improvement in lowland areas, and the difficulty of dating features belonging to acermanic periods. Nevertheless, we should also note that, within the context of the clauses, the terms *claud/foss* appear not to have referred to substantial monuments, although in one instance there is a reference to a 'great ditch' (*foss maur*) (Charter 240viii, Coe 2001: 1016-17). Indeed, some appear to have been drainage ditches or channels (e.g. Charter 218, Coe 2001: 701). Moreover, since many of the Llandaff estates were defined by the extent of the cultivated 'sharelands', it can be argued that some boundary dykes represent what are later described as *pen-cloddiau* ('head-dykes') (Seaman 2019a: 159). These were agricultural boundaries, also known as 'corn ditches', which separated permanently cultivated arable land ('infield') from the unenclosed pasture ('outfield') that was brought into cultivation more sporadically. These dykes were a feature of 'infield-outfield' farming systems across medieval Britain (Aston 1986: 127-30; Fleming and Ralph 1982: 105-6; Whittington 1973: 535). Where these survive, they can be identified on the ground comparatively easily, but their courses have often migrated over time and, again, they are notoriously difficult to date

(Austin 2016: 11). Many *pen-clawdd* must have been destroyed during the post-medieval period as arable expanded and common pastures were enclosed, but some are no doubt hiding in plain sight as part of present-day field systems.

Llywarch Hen's Dyke

In most of the boundary clauses in the *Book of Llandaff claud/foss* are used as common nouns for ditch/dyke features, but there are four instances where *claud* is compounded with a personal name to form a proper noun (Charters 123, 146, 155, 160). One of these, the *Claud Lyuarch hen* of Charter 146, stands out because of its direct allusion to Llywarch Hen, a pseudohistorical figure known independently of the place-name (Sims-Williams 1993: 51-54). The implications of this will be considered below, but first it is necessary to try and identify the dyke on the ground, before developing an understanding of the context of Llan-gors within the socio-political landscape of early medieval Wales.

Llywarch Hen's dyke is not recorded on any surviving maps of the Llan-gors area, so in order to locate the monument, the boundary clause of Charter 146 itself must be examined. Fortunately, this is quite detailed, and a number of features can be identified with some confidence (Campbell and Lane 1989: 679, Figure 1). A translation can be given as follows (features **emphasised** can be identified on the ground):

> From the mouth of the Spring of the Twelve Saints in **Llangorse Lake** upwards along the brook as far as the spring-head, to the end of Llywarch Hen's dyke. Along the dyke until it falls into the **river Llynfi**. Along it downwards as far as the end of Brynn Eital. Leftwards across to the end of the hill, to the source of the **Nant Tawel**. Along the stream as far as the **Llynfi**. Along the **Llynfi** as far as the **lake**. Along the lake as far as the mouth of the Spring of the Twelve Saints where it began (Coe 2001: 975-976).

This passage reveals that the dyke lies above Llangorse Lake, between the Spring of the Twelve Saints and the River Llyfi. The location of the spring, which is clearly a holy spring, is not recorded, but based on the direction of the perambulation and the rivers that are named it certainly rose and flowed into Llangorse Lake from the east (Seaman in press). Several brooks flow into Llangorse Lake from springs in this direction, but as discussed in another article, there is evidence to suggest that those identified on Figure 1 are the most likely candidates (Seaman in press). They all rise in the open pasture of Mynydd Llangorse, but are located just above the medieval parish boundary, which in this area follows a prominent *pen-clawdd* represented by substantial hollow-way and field-bank topped by a hedge that runs along the upper limit of the post-medieval enclosure (see Figures 3 and 4). The survival of this feature is intermittent, but its course can be followed for around 4km (depending upon which spring is identified as the holy spring). If this is the dyke then it must depart from the parish boundary if it is to 'fall into the Llynfi', and it is possible to trace a route that follows a lane and hollow-way through lower lying ground (see Figure 1). In this regard, it is relevant to note that *pen-clawdd* were often converted into lanes at points where they separated what were open fields from areas of shared pasture that have since been enclosed (Comeau 2012: 37; Fleming and Ralph 1982: 115). Thus, is it possible to identify a substantial *pen-clawdd* on the correct side of the Llangorse Lake, close to the likely location of the Spring of the Twelve Saints, which in large part follows the later parish boundary, and broadly matches the description given in the early medieval boundary clause. It is therefore suggested that this feature can be identified as Llywarch Hen's dyke. A potential problem with this interpretation is that the *pen-clawdd* circumnavigates the uplands of the Mynydd Troed, Mynydd Llangorse, and Cefn Moel to the south, and so it does not have a natural terminus. Nevertheless, the survival of the *pen-clawdd* is intermittent and trackways do cross its course close to all of the possible locations of the Spring of the Twelve Saints, so it could very well be that one of these was identified as a terminus when the bounds were written.

In the absence of any information from excavations it is very difficult to determine the date at which the dyke was constructed, but the system of infield-outfield agriculture to which it belonged is likely to have predated the early medieval period (cf. Cunliffe 2009: 57, 60). Indeed, its origins may lie in the early Roman period, when a record of sedimentation observed in a core taken from Llangorse Lake suggests there was an increase in woodland clearance and arable activity, indicating a related reorganization of farming systems at this time (Chambers 1999: 354-55; Jones *et al.* 1985: 229, 234).

In determining the location and identity of the Llywarch Hen's dyke, it is necessary to consider political history of Brycheiniog and the place of Llan-gors within the kingdom, since these are both relevant to the dyke's interpretation.

Llan-gors: a royal and ecclesiastical centre in Brycheiniog

The Llandaff charters suggest that kings had been active within Brycheiniog since the early eighth century, but it is not known if they were rulers *of* Brycheiniog or some other region at this time (Davies 1978: 18-20). The first reliable reference to kings of Brycheiniog is in the late ninth century *Life of Alfred the Great* where Asser recounts that 'Elise ap Tewdwr, king of Brycheiniog, being driven by the might of the same sons of Rhodri, sought of his own accord the lordship of King Alfred' (Keynes and Lapidge 1983: 96). Given that Asser's account suggests Elise ap Tewdwr's kingdom was under pressure from Gwynedd at the time he was writing, it is interesting to note that the Welsh annals record conflict between 'the men of Brycheiniog' and kingdom of Gwent in 848, whilst somewhat later the B and C texts of the *Anglo-Saxon Chronicle* record a Mercian raid on Brycheiniog in 916, in which the king's wife and thirty-three others was captured (Morris 1980: 48; Swanton 2000: 100).

The Mercian raid was focused on Llangorse Lake (described as *Brecenan mere* 'Brecon Mere'). The lake lies at the centre of a network of early routeways (Camden 1587: 357), and appears to have been the focus of a 'central zone' within Brycheiniog since at least the early eighth

Figure 3: Section of Llywarch Hen's Dyke, looking north. The open pastures of Mynydd Llan-gorse are to the right (©Peter Seaman)

century. Kings are associated with the Llan-gors area in Llandaff Charters 146, 167, and 237b (Seaman 2019b), and Alan Lane and Mark Redknap who conducted excavations on the unique ninth- to tenth-century crannog within Llangorse Lake, interpret the site as a

Figure 4: Llywarch Hen's dyke (topped with trees) running from left to right, with Llangorse Lake in the background. The second of the three springs marked on Figure 1, rises in the foreground and flows down towards the lake (©Peter Seaman)

Figure 5: The *pen-clawdd* demarcating the edge of the open pasture as seen from the south west side of the Llangorse Lake (©Peter Seaman).

royal residence and estate centre (see Figure 1). Indeed, they link the crannog's destruction and abandonment with the Mercian raid (Lane and Redknap in press). This central zone probably consisted of the later parishes of Llan-gors, Llanfihangel Tal-y-llyn (the subject of grants in Charters 167 and 237b), Cathedine, and Llangasty Talyllyn, all of which focus upon early churches. Llangasty Talyllyn is also associated with the eponymous royal dynasty of Brycheiniog in the *De Situ Brecheniauc and Cognacio Brychan*, two pseudohistorical texts which appear to have been created within early medieval Brycheiniog (Thomas 1994: 137-43). Also relevant to the royal status of Llan-gors and the mythology associated with its landscape are stories about Llangorse Lake recounted in the late twelve century by Gerald of Wales and Walter Map. In his *Journey Though Wales* Gerald describes how Gruffudd ap Rhys ap Tewdwr (d. 1137) declared and demonstrated that if the rightful prince of Wales commanded the birds of Llangorse Lake to sing, they would do so (Thorpe 1978: 93-95). Meanwhile, Map's *De Nugis Curialium* includes an early version of the 'Fairy Bride Legend', in which Brychan (the eponymous ruler of Brycheiniog) married a woman who emerged from Llangorse Lake (Wood 1992: 57). These stories are significant as they attest to an association between the landscape of Llan-gors and mythology related to kingship.

At some point after the Mercian raid, Llan-gors came into the possession of the Church. The evidence for this comes from the narration of Charter 237b (c. 929-944), which details how a dispute between a local king and bishop over food rents from the estate was resolved at the monastery at Llan-gors (Seaman 2019b). This monastery is likely to have been located at what is now the site of the parish church of St Paulinus, where three fragments of stone sculpture dating to between the ninth and twelfth centuries also attest to the significance of the site in the pre-Norman period (Redknap and Lewis 2007: 560-61). We know little about the estate after the mid-tenth century, but it may have been held by St David's before it was granted to Brecon Priory in the early twelfth century (Cowley 1977: 175). Brycheiniog ceased to exist as an independent kingdom sometime in the mid- to late tenth century, when it was subsumed into one of its neighbouring kingdoms (Davies 1982: 108).

Taken together, the evidence suggests that, during the ninth and tenth centuries at least, Brycheiniog was a 'frontier' kingdom with aggressors to the north, south, and east, and that Llan-gors was a centre of royal, and latterly ecclesiastical authority, which witnessed conflict and incursion on at least one occasion.

Place-stories in the early medieval landscape

Llywarch Hen was purportedly a sixth-century ruler in the 'Old North' (Williams 1935), but it was not the historical Llywarch whose name was invoked in the *Claud Lyuarch hen*. In early medieval Wales, Llywarch Hen was known primarily through a substantial body of poetry composed well after the historical figure's death (Rowland 1990). Llywarch is not the only figure from the Old North who was transplanted into the early medieval Welsh landscape through oral literary tradition. Others, such as

Owain ab Urien and Cynon ap Clydno Eidyn, are localised in a Welsh geographical context in the *Englynion y Beddau* (The Stanzas of the Graves) (Petts 2007: 164). Similarly, elsewhere in the *Book of Llandaff*, a place-name in Charter 206, *Messur Prituenn*, alludes to the story of *Culhwch ac Olwen* (Coe 2001: 597-98). It is not surprising that the name of a dyke should reference a figure from oral tradition, since there was a strong association between place and narrative in the early medieval world (MacCana 1988). The clearest articulation of this phenomenon is found in the *dindshenchas* collections of early Irish prose and poetry that recount place-names and the mythological narratives attached to them (Gwynn 1991), but numerous instances are encountered in medieval Welsh literature; such as in the *Mabinogi* and the *De Situ Brecheniauc* (Bollard 2009; Petts 2007; Siewers 2005). What we see here is a reflection of the importance attributed to places, their names, and the onomastic tales that preserved and perpetuated them in the ordering of landscape by societies with few written records and no maps. In pre-literate societies, place-names survived through oral tradition, and as 'place-stories' became fixed in the landscape. In this fashion, the oral tradition came to construct the identity of that place, and vice-versa. This process helped to establish a 'sense of place' for people within their landscapes (Gardiner 2012: 21; Tilley 1994: 18). Moreover, anthropological studies have demonstrated how place-stories rooted in the fabric of the landscape accrued ideological significance and had the power to perpetuate tradition and engender particular understandings of the world through the establishment of social norms (Basso 1996: 77-104; *cf.* Johnson 2007: 148-49). Thus, John Bollard (2009) has examined how place-names and the landscape were 'central characters' in the *Mabinogi*, which served as reminders both of the cultural significance of the tales and of the importance of the themes they explore (see also Siewers (2005: 197) who sees the *Mabinogi* as a 'dynamic dialogue of Otherworld and topography'). Similarly, Alex Woolf (2008) has argued that the moral of a story in the *Historia Brittonum* where the citadel of the unjust and tyrannical King Benllie is destroyed through divine providence was referenced in the landscape through the juxtaposition of Moel Fenlli ('Bare hill of Benllie' an Iron Age hillfort) and Llanarmon Yn Ial (an commotal centre of Powys). Particularly relevant to the present study is David Petts's analysis of the ninth- or tenth-century poems recorded in the *Englynion y Beddau* (The Stanzas of the Graves) (Petts 2007). Petts argues that the three-line verses of the poem served to 'connect the contemporary landscape to a perceived, mythical past' through the localization of the burial places of mythological individuals within the Welsh landscape. Indeed, some of the burial locations can be identified with prehistoric monuments, whose original construction, like that of Llywarch's dyke at Llan-gors, was lost to time (Petts 2007: 164-5). Importantly, Petts argues that this mythologisation of the landscape should be seen within the socio-political context of the time in which the stanzas were written. Noting that alongside the pressure being exerted on the Welsh by the Vikings and the Anglo-Saxon kingdoms during the ninth and tenth centuries, 'the poem transforms the landscape of Wales with its landmarks, both natural and prehistoric, into a landscape of resistance to Saxon and Danish incursions' (Petts 2007: 165).

The affective nature of place-stories reflected in early medieval oral and literary tradition was particularly important in the definition of boundaries. In a world without maps, territorial boundaries, particularly those that were contested, had to be inscribed upon the physical landscape through the cultural memory of its inhabitants (Gardiner 2012: 21-22). The boundaries of estates were reinforced through their perambulation and the performance of rituals and recounting of stories, in front of witnesses, at particular points along the processual route (Howe 2008: 37-39). When these 'oral performances' of property rights and transactions were written down as charters the central importance of names and places was such that 'the vernacular had to bleed through the Latin text' (Geary 1999: 176). It is for this reason that whilst the text of early medieval charters was usually written in Latin, the boundary clauses were more often in the vernacular, so that when they were performed aloud the place-stories they referenced could be understood by lay audiences (Geary 1999: 177-81; Kelly 1990: 56-57). The names of boundary features and the oral traditions associated with them formed the 'mnemonic pegs' that gave structure to this process of memorisation. For the most part the onomastic tales associated with early medieval boundary features do not survive, but since Llywarch Hen's dyke was associated with a body of oral tradition, some of which was later written down, it provides an opportunity explore the confluence of a place, name, and narrative.

Llywarch Hen's Lament: poetry in a contested landscape

The Llywarch Hen poems survive in documents of the thirteenth century and later, but the material or at least some of it, is thought to have been composed in the eighth or ninth century (Rowland 1990: 388-89; for a translation see Koch 2003: 385-404). Several places in Brycheiniog can be identified in the poetry, and Patrick Sims-Williams (1993) has argued that it was composed at Llan-gors. In this regard, it may be significant that the Llan-gors dyke is one of a number of features associated Llywarch within Brycheiniog, others include the Llyn (lake), Nant (stream), Bedd (grave – which appears to be a reference to a prehistoric standing stone), and Waun (moor) of Llywarch (Llywelyn 2018: 20; 77, 88, 112). Two sets of verses can be distinguished within the poetry, both of which are narrated from the perspective of Llywarch Hen. The first takes the form of a dialogue between Llywarch and Gwen, his last surviving son, in which Llywarch goads Gwen into unwise, and ultimately fatal, battle. The second set forms a lament, in which the aging Llywarch bemoans his foolish actions and fading abilities as a warrior. The narrative context of the verses would have been known to its original audience but is lost in a modern context. It is therefore difficult to interpret the meaning the poetry and the oral traditions they arose out of, but we can be sure that this was not praise poetry; Llywarch's story is about the violation of social norms, and the verses comes across as a warning rather than exemplar (Charles-Edwards 2013: 668-74; Rowland 2014: xviii-xxii). Indeed, the themes recounted in the poetry, such as inter-British feuding, battles against the Anglo-Saxons, and the defence of borders, resonate with Llan-gors, its likely place of composition, since during the late ninth and early tenth centuries Llan-gors was a royal estate in a frontier kingdom threatened by Gwynedd and Gwent and raided by the Mercians at least once. Whilst the moral of Llywarch's tale is difficult to reconstruct, it is noteworthy that a central verse of the surviving poetry refers to Gwen's (the last surviving son of Llywarch Hen) last stand against the Anglo-Saxons at the 'Battle of the Green Dyke' (¶67). Perhaps, therefore, it was this story that was alluded to through Llywarch's dyke. In this regard it may not be coincidence that Llywarch Hen's dyke defined the eastern and northern sides of the estate at Llan-gors, which is the direction from which an English attack would have come in 916 (Sims-Williams 1993: 53).

It can be confidently assumed that antecedents of the surviving Llywarch Hen poetry were recounted at Llan-gors, perhaps within a hall on the crannog or during open air festivals when the freemen of the region gathered 'to sing songs, recite their pedigrees, hear tales of the heroism of their ancestors' (Davies 1987: 80). Onomastic tales associated with Llywarch Hen were no doubt also performed at the dyke during the perambulation of the estate's bounds and as people and animals crossed the dyke during seasonal patterns of movement. By narrating Llywarch's story through the landscape and rooting it in the concrete details of the dyke, an ancient feature that formed that the backbone of the agriculture landscape, the tales and the dyke acquired mythic value and historic relevance (Bollard 2009: 40; Tilley 1994: 33). Thus, it can be suggested that the dyke and Llywarch's lament that was told through it served as a didactic that enforced knowledge of the physical extent of the estate, but also the status and perhaps the obligations and responsibilities of the royal dynasty who held it. The dyke was not then an overtly defensive 'military' earthwork, and it was certainly not built by Llywarch Hen, neither was it simply an agricultural boundary and a convenient feature with which to construct a boundary clause; but as a narrative site of battle, it was a mnemonic peg that both physically and metaphorically defined a centre of power and authority.

Llywarch Hen's dyke should, therefore, be set alongside the body folklore focused on Llan-gors that was later recounted by Gerald of Wales and Walter Map. It is unknown why the association with Llywarch Hen arose within Brycheiniog at this time. Llywarch does not appear in the genealogy of the royal dynasty and was not an ancestral figure, but if Llywarch's role within the poetry was to demonstrate the folly of unwise leadership it may be significant that he was claimed as an ancestor by the kings of Gwynedd who, as demonstrated, were pressuring Brycheiniog at the time of its composition (Maund 2006: 48).

Saints and sinners: Christianizing boundaries

As demonstrated above, the boundary clause of Charter 146 records that Llywarch Hen's dyke was adjacent to a feature described as the 'Spring of the Twelve Saints'

('Finnaun y Dodec Seint'). This holy spring was most likely dedicated to the Twelve Apostles, whose cult was propagated in South Wales during the tenth and eleventh centuries (Seaman in press). The spring and its waters may have offered spiritual protection to animals and people as they travelled into and out of the estate. It was no doubt also associated with a body of oral tradition that operated in a similar way to the Llywarch Hen poetry, However, there may be more to the juxtaposition of the spring and dyke than first appears. Explicitly Christian features are generally rare in early medieval boundary clauses, and John Blair (2005: 488) has argued that 'boundary perambulation was still, in the late tenth and early eleventh centuries, essentially a secular activity which had not yet assimilated into liturgical ritual'. Thus, it is likely that the Spring of the Twelve Saints, or at least the spring's Christian associations, was a comparatively late addition to an earlier boundary clause. This may be significant, since the estate came into the possession of the Church sometime after the Mercian raid of 916 at broadly same the time the cult of the Twelve Apostles were being propagated in the region (Seaman in press). The secular themes of Llywarch's story would no doubt have been unpalatable to the Church, but since they were part of how the estate was inscribed in cultural memory they could not be easily erased or forgotten. Therefore, we may suggest, speculatively, that the juxtaposition of spring and dyke could represent a comparatively late attempt to Christianize the bounds of the estate and the stories associated with them.

Conclusions

Dykes and ditches must have been common features within both the upland and lowland landscapes of early medieval Wales, but they have scarcely attracted the scholarly attention they deserve. Indeed, it is very likely that many early medieval (and earlier) *pen-clawdd* lie unnoticed within the countryside of Wales today. The evidence suggests that a range of dyke types were to be found in the early medieval landscape, and targeted research, including survey and excavation is needed to understand their different functions. Hopefully, however, this paper demonstrates how a multidisciplinary approach can help to also understand something of how dykes were engaged with as 'places' operating as mnemonic pegs in the early medieval landscape.

Acknowledgements

The ideas for this article developed after Alan Lane invited the author to write a discussion of the Llan-gors charter material for the publication of the crannog excavations. I am very grateful for this opportunity and Alan's encouragement and critical insight. My ideas have benefited greatly from discussions with Rhiannon Comeau and Mike Bintley, and I would like to thank Peter Seaman and Nicola Emmerson for helping with identifying (and walking) the bounds and photographing the dyke.

Bibliography

Arnold, C. and Davies, J. 2000. *Roman and Early Medieval Wales.* Stroud: Sutton.

Aston, M. 1986. *Interpreting the Landscape: Landscape Archaeology and Local History.* Routledge: London.

Austin, D. 2016. Reconstructing the upland landscapes of medieval Wales. *Archaeologia Cambrensis* 165: 1–20.

Basso, K. 1996. *Wisdom Sits in Places.* Albuquerque: University of New Mexico Press.

Blair, J. 2005. *The Church in Anglo-Saxon Society.* Cambridge: Cambridge University Press.

Bollard, J.K. 2009. Landscapes of *The Mabinogi. Landscapes* 10(2): 37-60.

Brooke, C. 1986. *The Church and the Welsh Border in the Central Middle Ages.* Woodbridge: Boydell.

Camden, W. 1587. *Britannia siue Florentissimorum regnorum, Angliae, Scotiae, Hiberniae, et insularum adiacentium ex intima antiquitate chorographica description.* London.

Campbell, E. and Lane, A. 1989. Llangorse: a 10th century Royal Crannog in Wales. *Antiquity* 63: 673–681.

Chambers, F. 1999. The Quaternary history of Llangorse Lake: implications for conservation. *Aquatic Conservation: Marine and Freshwater Ecosystems* 9: 343-59.

Charles-Edwards, T. 2013. *Wales and the Britons 350-1064.* Oxford: Oxford University Press.

Coe, J. 2001. The Place-Names of the Book of Llandaf. Unpublished thesis: University of Wales Aberystwyth.

Coe, J. 2004. Dating the Boundary Clauses in the Book of Llandaff. *Cambrian Medieval Celtic Studies* 48: 1–43.

Comeau, R. 2012. From Tregordd to Tithe: identifying settlement patterns in a north Pembrokeshire parish. *Landscape History* 33(1): 29–44.

Cowley, F. 1977. *The Monastic Order in South Wales 1066–1349.* Cardiff: University of Wales Press.

Crampton, C. 1966. An interpretation of the pollen and sols in cross-ridge dykes of Glamorgan. *Bulletin of the Board of Celtic Studies* 21(4): 376–90.

Cunliffe, B. 2009. *Iron Age Communities in Britain* 4th ed. London: Routledge.

Davies, J. 2003. *The Book of Llandaff and the Norman Church.* Woodbridge: Boydell.

Davies, R.R. 1987. *The Conquest: Wales, 1063–1415.* Oxford: Oxford University Press.

Davies, W. 1978. *An Early Welsh Microcosm.* London: Royal Historical Society.

Davies, W. 1979. *The Llandaff Charters.* Aberystwyth: The National Library of Wales.

Davies, W. 1982. *Wales in the Early Middle Ages.* Leicester: Leicester University Press.

Edwards, N. (ed.) 1997. *Landscape and Settlement in Medieval Wales.* Oxford: Oxbow.

Edwards, N., Davies, T. and Hemer, K. 2017. Research Framework for the Archaeology of Early Medieval Wales. https://archaeoleg.org.uk/pdf/review2017/earlymedreview2017.pdf

Evans, J.G. and Rhys, J. 1979. *The Text of the Book of Llan Dâv*. Aberystwyth: National Library of Wales.

Fleming A. and Ralph, N. 1982. Medieval settlement and land use on Holne Moor, Dartmoor: the landscape evidence. *Medieval Archaeology* 26: 101–37.

Fox, C. 1955. *Offa's Dyke*. London: British Academy.

Gardiner, M. 2012. Oral tradition, landscape and the social life of place-names. In Jones, R. and Semple, S. eds. *Sense of Place in Anglo-Saxon England*. Donington: Shaun Tyas: 16–30.

Geary, P.J. 1999. Land, language and memory in Europe 700-1100. *Transactions of the Royal Historical Society*, 6th series, 9: 169–84.

Gwynn. E.J. 1991. *The Metrical Dindshenchas*. Dublin: Dublin Institute for Advanced Studies.

Hankinson, R. and Caseldine, A. 2006. Short dykes in Powys and their origins. *Archaeological Journal* 163: 264-69.

Howe, N. 2008. *Writing the Map of Anglo-Saxon England: Essays in Cultural Geography*. Yale: Yale University Press.

Johnson, M. 2007. *Ideas of Landscape*. Oxford: Blackwell.

Jones, R., Benson-Evans, K. and Chambers, F. 1985. Human influence upon sedimentation in Llangorse Lake, Wales. *Earth Surface Processes and Landforms* 10: 1377–82.

Kelly, S. 1990. Anglo-Saxon lay society and the written word. In R. McKitterick ed. *The Uses of Literacy in Early Medieval Europe*: 36-62. Cambridge: Cambridge University Press.

Keynes, S. and Lapidge, M. 1983. *Alfred the Great: Asser's Life of King Alfred and other contemporary sources*. London: Penguin.

Koch, J.T. 2003. *The Celtic Heroic Age: Literary Sources for Ancient Celtic Europe and Early Ireland and Wales*. Aberystwyth: Celtic Studies Publications.

Lane, A. and Redknap, M. 2019. *The Llangorse Crannog: An Early Medieval Island Residence of the Kings of Brycheiniog*. Oxford: Oxbow.

Lewis, R. 2006. Cross Ridge Dykes of southeast Wales: Survey and Excavation. GGAT report no. 2006.103. Swansea: GGAT.

Llywelyn, M. 2018. *Place Names in the Brecon Beacons National Park*. Llanrwst: Gwasg Garreg Gwalch.

MacCana, P. 1988. Placenames and mythology in Irish tradition: places, pilgrimages, and things. In G. W. Mac Lennan (ed.) *Proceedings of the First North American Congress of Celtic Studies*. Ottawa: University of Ottawa: 319–41.

Maldonado, A. 2015. The early medieval Antonine Wall. *Britannia* 46: 225–45.

Maund, K. 2006. *The Welsh Kings: Warriors, Warlords and Princes*. Stroud: Tempus.

Morris, J. 1980. *Nennius, British History and the Welsh Annals*. London: Phillimore.

Petts, D. 2007. *De Situ Brecheniauc* and *Englynion Y Beddau*: writing about burial in early medieval Wales. *Anglo-Saxon Studies in Archaeology and History* 14: 163-72.

RCAHMW 1976. *An Inventory of the Ancient Monuments in Glamorgan, Volume I: Pre-Norman, Part III, The Early Christian Period.* Cardiff: HMSO.

Redknap, M. and Lewis, J. 2007. *A Corpus of Early Medieval Inscribed Stones and Stone Sculpture in Wales: Volume I.* Cardiff: University of Wales Press.

Rowland, J. 1990. *Early Welsh Saga Poetry: A Study and Edition of the Englynion.* Woodbridge: Brewer.

Rowland, J. 2014. *A Selection of Early Welsh Saga Poems.* London: Modern Humanities Research Association.

Seaman, A. 2019a. Landscape, settlement and agriculture in early medieval Brycheiniog: the evidence from the Llandaff Charters, in R. Comeau and A. Seaman (eds) *Living off the Land: Agriculture in Wales c. 400 to 1600 AD.* Oxford: Windgather: 153-73.

Seaman, A. 2019b. The Llangorse charter material, in A. Lane and M. Redknap *The Llangorse Crannog: An Early Medieval Island Residence of the Kings of Brycheiniog.* Oxford: Oxbow: 414-21.

Seaman, A. in press. Finnaun y Doudec Seint: A Holy Spring in the Early Medieval Kingdom of Brycheiniog, in C. Ray (ed.) *Sacred Springs and Holy Wells: A Cross-Cultural Compendium.* London: Routledge.

Siewers, A.K. 2005. Writing an icon of the land: the *Mabinogi* as a mystagogy of landscape. *Peritia* 19: 193-228.

Silvester, R. and Hankinson, R. 2002. The Short Dykes of Mid and North-East Wales. CPAT report no. 458. Welshpool: CPAT.

Sims-Williams, P. 1993. The provenance of the Llywarch Hen Poems: a case for Llan-gors, Brycheiniog. *Cambrian Medieval Celtic Studies* 26: 27–63.

Swanton, M. 2000. *The Anglo-Saxon Chronicles.* London: Phoenix.

Thomas, C. 1994. *And Shall these Mute Stones Speak? Post-Roman Inscriptions in Western Britain.* Cardiff: University of Wales Press.

Thorpe, L. 1978. *The Journey through Wales; and The Description of Wales, by Gerald of Wales.* London: Penguin.

Tilley, C. 1994. *A Phenomenology of Landscape: Places, Paths and Monuments.* Oxford: Berg.

Watson, M. 2002. *Shropshire: An Archaeological Guide.* Shrewsbury: Shropshire Books.

Whittington, G. 1973. Field systems of Scotland, in A. R. H. Baker and R. A. Butler (eds) *Studies of Field Systems in The British Isles.* Cambridge: Cambridge University Press: 530–79.

Williams, I. 1935. *Canu Llywarch Hen.* Cardiff: University of Wales Press.

Wood, J. 1992. The fairy bride legend in Wales. *Folklore* 103 (1): 56-72.

Woolf, A. 2008. Fire from heaven: divine providence and Iron Age hillforts in early medieval Britain, in P. Rainbird (ed.) *Monuments in the Landscape.* Stroud: History Press: 136-43.

Andy Seaman, Senior Lecturer, School of Humanities, Canterbury Christ Church University
Email: andy.seaman@canterbury.ac.uk

The Danevirke:
Preliminary Results of New Excavations
(2010–2014) at the Defensive System in the
German-Danish Borderland

Astrid Tummuscheit and Frauke Witte

Between 2010 and 2014, the State Archaeological Department of Schleswig-Holstein in Germany jointly undertook excavation work with the Danish Museum Sønderjylland – Arkæologi Haderslev on the linear earthwork monument, the Danevirke. These transnational excavations have led to important new findings, which include the discovery of the site of a gateway, where major transport routes converged for at least five hundred years. Furthermore, newly gained C14-dates indicate that the second main building phase of the Danevirke dates to around AD 500. Therefore, the dating of the first beginnings of the earthwork must be pushed back in time, making the Danevirke more than 200 years older than previously thought. Additionally, dendrochronological dates show that around the year AD 1200 substantial building activities took place, which reveal the intention of developing the Danevirke further. A project is currently ongoing, which aims to publish the results of the 2010-2014 excavations. This article outlines the synopsis of those results and current working hypotheses.

Keywords: Danevirke, Hedeby (Haithabu), Jutland, Schlei fjord, Schleswig, UNESCO

> Perhaps no other linear barrier demonstrates such development over such a long period of time (Spring 2015: 114)

The Danevirke

In the southern part of the Jutland Peninsula, in what is now northern Germany, a system of earthworks, palisades and stone walls form the 'Deed of the Danes' otherwise known as the Danevirke in Danish, or Danewerk in German (Figure 1). The excavation site is in Germany, located in the former duchy of Schleswig, about 5km south-west of its historic capital the town of Schleswig (Figures 2 and 3).[1] The area has been Danish-German borderland since at least the early Middle Ages and was within Denmark until the Danish-Prussian war of 1864. Together with the trading site of Hedeby the Danevirke was inscribed by UNESCO as a World Heritage Site in June 2018.

The Danevirke has a total length measuring around 32km and was constructed in several phases across the narrowest section of the Jutland Peninsula (Figures 1 and 2). It stretches from the low-lying wetlands of the North Sea coast in the west of the peninsula to the east, where the Schlei fjord, a narrow inlet of the Baltic Sea, reaches inland as far as the town of Schleswig, thus constricting the north-south land route to a 6km-wide zone at

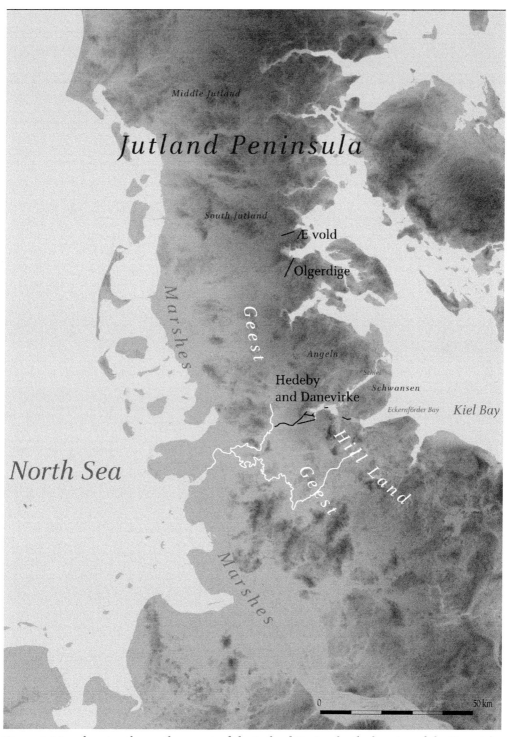

Figure 1: Map showing the southern part of the Jutland Peninsula, the location of the Danevirke at the Isthmus of Schleswig and other linear earthworks mentioned in the text (after Maluck and Weltecke 2016: 58-59 with additions).

Table 1: the relationship between German, Danish and English terms for components of the Danevirke

German	Danish	English
Hauptwall	Hovedvolden	Main Rampart
Krummwall	Krumvolden	Crooked Rampart
Nordwall	Nordvolden	North Rampart
Osterwall	Østervolden	East Rampart
Halbkreiswall	Halvkredsvolden	Semicircular Rampart
Verbindungswall	Forbindelsesvolden	Connection Rampart
Kograben	Kovirket	Kovirke
Doppelwall	Dobbeltvolden	Double Rampart
Bogenwall	Buevolden	Curved Rampart
Seesperrwerk Reesholm	Stegsvig Søspærringen	Offshore work Reesholm
Feldsteinmauer	Kampestensmuren	Fieldstone Wall
Sodenwall	Tørvemuren	Turf Wall
Waldemarsmauer	Waldemarsmuren	Brick Wall
Palisadenwall	Palisadevolden	Palisade
Haithabu	Hedeby	Hedeby
Ochsenweg	Hærvejen	Ox Road or Army Road

Figure 2 (previous page): The Danevirke has a total length of about 32km and was constructed in several phases across the neck of the Jutland Peninsula. The site of the 2010-2014 excavation (red dot) is located about 5km south-west of the town of Schleswig (after Maluck and Weltecke 2016: 66-67).

Figure 3: The excavation site in 2013 as seen from the east. The Main Rampart of the Danevirke runs from south-west to north-east. Today it is crossed by a modern road named 'Ochsenweg'. At the excavation site one can see the remains of the Fieldstone Wall, which has a wide gap, which is the site of the former gate. There is also the section through the Main Rampart (for details see Figure 6).

the *Schleswiger Landenge* (Isthmus of Schleswig). During its period of use which reaches roughly from the time around AD 500 to AD 1250, the structure was enhanced, reinforced and rebuilt several times to adapt it to new political and military requirements (Figure 4). The Danevirke consists of several earthen ramparts, a stone wall dating to the eighth century and a twelfth-century monumental brick wall (Figure 5), not to mention its reuse in the nineteenth and twentieth centuries.[2]

The 5.4km-long Main Rampart (Hauptwall) is the core of the system. It includes all building phases (including a fieldstone wall and a brick wall) originating from sometime before AD 500 to around AD 1250. At the site of the 2010-2014 excavation, the Main Rampart is crossed by the ancient trackway known as either Hærvejen (the Army Road) or Ochsenweg (Ox Road). This route runs north-south across the spine of the Jutland Peninsula from the Limfjord area in the north to the River Elbe in the south. It dates back to at least the Bronze

---

[2]   If not cited otherwise, the following description of the different parts of the Danevirke is based on Andersen's monograph (Andersen 1998; Hamann 1861; Müller and Neergaard 1903; La Cour 1951; Maluck 2017; in English, see also Dobat 2005, 2008).

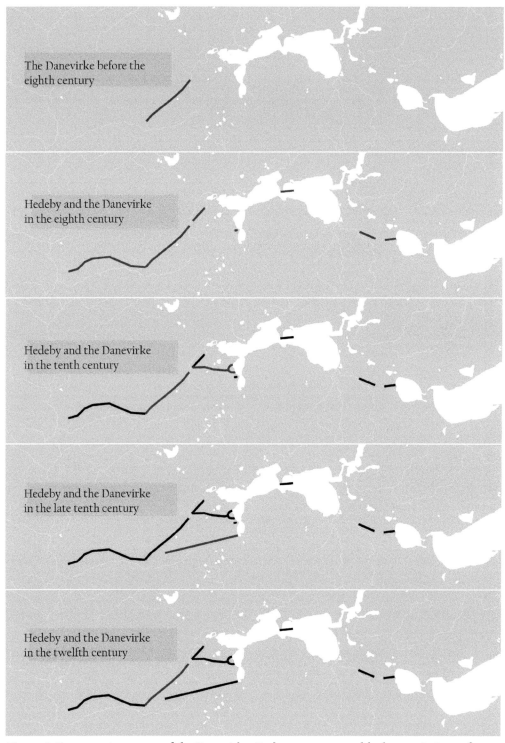

The Danevirke before the eighth century

Hedeby and the Danevirke in the eighth century

Hedeby and the Danevirke in the tenth century

Hedeby and the Danevirke in the late tenth century

Hedeby and the Danevirke in the twelfth century

Figure 4: Construction stages of the Danevirke. Red are new stages, black are existing or former stages, some of which may have persisted in use into subsequent centuries (after Maluck and Weltecke 2016: 91).

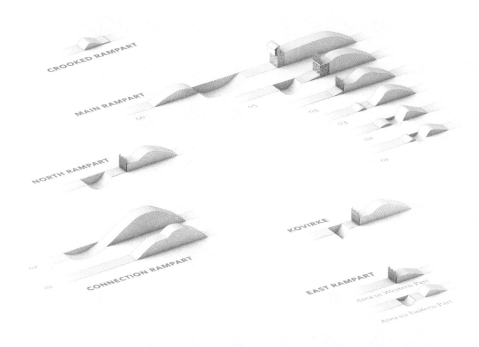

Figure 5: Building phases of the different parts of the Danevirke (Maluck and Weltecke 2016: 76-77 after Andersen 2004).

Age but may have earlier origins (Becker-Christensen 1981; Madsen 2018).

On the western flank of the Main Rampart the 6.6km-long Crooked Rampart (Krummwall) runs on the northern side of the Rheider Au valley as far as the medieval harbour of Hollingstedt on the River Treene in the west. As far as we know at present, the Crooked Rampart was added around AD 700 to the Main Rampart.

The North Rampart (Nordwall) is a 1.7km-long north-eastern extension to the Main Rampart. It reaches as far as the innermost part of the Schlei fjord. The North Rampart as well as the wooden offshore work Reesholm (Sperrwerk) (1.8km) were dated by dendrochronology to the years around AD 740.[3] Due to the similarities in construction it can be deduced that the East Rampart (Osterwall) was built around the same time. Furthermore, the Main Rampart was strengthened around the same time period, or later, by the addition of a stone wall.

After a long break in activity, building activities resumed during the tenth century when the Semicircular Rampart was constructed to protect the harbour and trading centre of Hedeby (Haithabu). Shortly after, the 4km-long Connection Rampart

---

[3] There are more earthworks belonging to the Danevirke system such as the Double Rampart or the Curved Rampart (Andersen 1998: 110–117), which are excluded in this brief overview.

(Verbindungswall) was added to link Hedeby with the Danevirke system for the first time. At the end of the tenth century, the 6.5km-long straight line of the Kovirke (Kograben) was erected south of the old Danevirke line, forming an additional protection to Hedeby's southern approaches.

Both the Connection Rampart and the Kovirke can be attributed to the Danish King Harald Bluetooth (c. AD 910–987). These can also be understood as a general display of royal power, but in particular it is a strong claim to Hedeby, making it so the settlement apparently no longer lay south of the Danevirke – no doubt for protective reasons, but possibly because of legal implications.[4] In the late twelfth century, the Danish King Waldemar I (the Great) instructed a monumental brick wall to be built in front of the Danevirke, which introduced brick as a new building material to the feature over at least 4km of the Main Rampart.

Excavations 2010-2014

When excavations started in 2010, a 5-6m wide gap was found, which later proved to be the remains of the opening where the Ox Road/Army Road originally crossed the Main Rampart of the Danevirke (Tummuscheit 2011: 84-87: Tummuscheit and Witte 2014a, 2014b) (Figure 2). Surely, as this was one main crossing point of the earthwork it is likely that it is the site of the gate mentioned in the Royal Frankish Annals in the year AD 808 (Scholz 1972) (Figure 3).

During the following years, the main focus was on the investigation of this possible gate and passageway through the earthwork. A large section through the entire rampart was also examined which included its earliest building phases, as well as excavation of a large area which lies south of and in front of the rampart and gate (Figures 3 and 6). One of the central aims of the excavation and the current post-excavation work is to gain a better understanding of the Danevirke's chronology, in order to relate the site's history and development to specific historical events.

The oldest phases (Phase 1/2 and 3)

It is commonly understood that the oldest part of the Main Rampart has a sequence of two building phases, a result derived mainly from excavations by Günther Haseloff in the 1930s (Haseloff 1937) and Hellmuth Andersen in the 1990s (Andersen 1998). The recent excavation has shown, however, that this rampart was probably constructed more or less in one main phase using the same building technique (Phase 1/2).[5]

The oldest earthwork (Phase 1/2) consists of sandy layers upon a cultural layer. The original ground surface (Figure 6) was removed over almost the entire excavated area,

---

[4]   For more information about Harald Bluetooth works and the settlement of Hedeby, see e.g. Jensen 2006 and Jankuhn 1986.

[5]   Traditionally termed phase 1 and 2 of the Main Rampart as in Figure 5.

probably to be used for the stabilization of the top of the wall. In the cultural layer there were post-holes and plough-marks. No material suitable for radiocarbon dating was found in these ramparts or the cultural layer. To the south, right in front of the wall, was a ditch belonging to this phase. It was about 2.8 m wide and only about 0.5 m deep.

It was not possible to extend the excavation area to where the gateway crosses the oldest earthen phase (Phase 1/2), because it is on private property. It does seem though that the rampart was considerably lower than it is a few hundred metres to the west, which could be a vague indication of some sort of disruption of the earthworks in this area rather than variation in its original design.

The turf wall is the second main phase of the Main Rampart, traditionally termed Phase 3 (Figures 5 and 6). It was placed in front (south) of the oldest earthwork and on top of the earliest ditch. In the gate area, both endings of this second rampart, definitely have a purpose-built gap, showing that a gate or opening already existed by this early stage, if not demonstrably in Phase 1/2 (Figure 7).

As this fortification was made of burnt heather turf, five samples were taken in order to determine radiocarbon dates for its construction (see Tummuscheit and Witte 2013: 146-66, 2014a, 2014b). The results revealed a date around the fifth and sixth centuries AD (Holst 2013: 147-48). Two sixth-century dates may hint that the wall was made taller sometime after the building of the wall. There had been suggestions of an early dating of the Danevirke among scholars before (i.e. Harck 1998; Madsen 2008: 40), but until the new radiocarbon dates there was no direct evidence for it and the generally accepted view was that the upstanding element of the Danevirke began c. AD 700 (e.g. Dobat 2008: 38-40). This early dating of the Danevirke means that the origins of the monument need to be fundamentally reassessed and we must re-evaluate the context in which it was first established. In particular, the origins of the Danevirke (fifth century) and the origins of the settlement of Hedeby (middle/late eighth century) cannot be connected any longer ('initial phase': Dobat 2008: 48). This also means that the theories of pressure from the Slavonic immigration and potential threat from the Frankish Empire can no longer serve as a possible impetus for constructing the first rampart, although these factors remain potential contexts prompting the later large enhancements and reinforcements to the Danevirke some hundred years later (Dobat 2008: 50).

As written sources are generally scarce for this early period, coupled with the fact their reliability can be questionable, it is generally considered that there is some sort of centralized leadership at this time.[6] Both the archaeological and the written sources give hints on the interaction between the Jutes or Danes and the Angles (Ethelberg 2012: 286-300; Ethelberg 2017: 15-27), which might have led to the building of the first rampart.

---

[6] These questions are part of the ongoing research in the project. The engagement with the subject will give new insights into the socio-political organization of southern Scandinavia in the future.

Figure 6: A large section through the early Danevirke rampart north of the Fieldstone Wall looking south-west

Figure 7: The ending of the Turf Wall on the western side of the gate as seen from the north-east

Why would there be an interest in building a more than 5 km-long earthwork – phases 1/2 and 3 of the Main Rampart – close to or around AD 500 anyway? Taking into account local typology, changes in burial rites, evidence of other ramparts further north (e.g. Olgerdiget, Æ vold: Figure 1) and finds from weapon sacrifices, one can imagine that as the Angles pressed northwards in the course of founding an early state around the first century AD (Ethelberg 2012). Two ramparts facing north were constructed (banks, palisades and ditches: Olgerdiget at AD 31 and Æ vold at around AD 150), forcing the inhabitants of this area to move further north. At some point these people reclaimed the land, pressing the Angles to the south again, and eventually erecting the main rampart of the Danevirke (Witte 2017: 5). At this time the identity of this group is unknown, it is possible it was one of the groups known from written sources (Dorey 1969; Gudeman 1900) of the first century AD, such as 'Jutes', 'the Varian tribe' or 'Danes' (Ethelberg 2017: 15-17, 27).

Palisade and Fieldstone Wall (Phase 4/5)

It is a still a matter of debate if the Fieldstone Wall represents Phase 4 (Kramer 1984: 346) or Phase 5 (Andersen 2004: 24) of the Main Rampart (Kramer 1984; Andersen 1985; Andersen 1998: 49, 171; Tummuscheit and Witte 2018: 71). The central problem is whether posts, which repeatedly appear in connection with the wall, are the remains of a palisade and therefore represent an independent building in Phase 4 (Figure 5) or if they are an inherent part of the wall itself (Phase 5).

Originally, the Fieldstone Wall was 3m high, 3m wide and up to 4km long (Figure 8). It is a 'Shell wall' (in German 'Schalenmauer'[7]) built of fieldstones or small boulders.[8] Especially at the front and the back, the stones were laid repeatedly in a herringbone pattern while the interior was built throughout of clay and rubble. At the back, the wall was always cut into the older earthworks and it had an additional support made of clean yellow clay. It is therefore evident that the herringbone pattern was not applied for aesthetical reasons, but to improve the stability.

Similarly to earlier phases the gateway survives, and west of this gate, the wall was comparatively poorly preserved, as it was used as a quarry to gather stones for the foundation of the brick built Waldemarsmauer in the late twelfth century (Figure 8 and 10). In the 2010-2014 excavation the Fieldstone Wall was found to sit partly on the remains of the Turf Rampart and the underlying fill of the earliest ditch (Figures 6 and 10).[9]

The aforementioned characteristic row of substantial post-holes (one approximately every 2m) were found under the base of the Fieldstone Wall. In some places there is evidence that the wall was built with the posts still standing. The posts were therefore interpreted by Kramer (1984) as a structural element belonging to the monument itself and not to an older palisade as Andersen believed (Andersen 1998: 171 ff.). Consequently, the dendrochronological dates of wooden remains in some of these post-holes were used to date the wall to around AD 740 (Kramer 1984). As similar dendrochronological dates were gained in other parts of the Danevirke it has, for the last decades however, been widely agreed that the wall was part of a huge construction project dating from shortly before AD 740 (Kramer 1984), this also included the reinforcement of the Main Rampart, the erection of the North Rampart, the wooden offshore work at Reesholm and the East Rampart (Kramer 1992; Kramer 1995) (Figure 4).

Although the phase following the Turf Wall (Phase 3 of the Main Rampart see Figure 5) was difficult to detect in the excavation, the current hypothesis, that Andersen put forth, holds up; that the row of posts represents remains of a wooden palisade which was erected in around AD 740 as an independent building phase (which would then represent Phase 4 of the Main Rampart see Figure 5) and which only some decades

---

[7]   The German word 'Schalenmauer' translates as 'Cavity Wall' the construction is not unlike a drystone wall, with larger stones on the exterior of the wall, with the center packed with smaller loose stones and mortar. Here the term Shell Wall will be used to describe this.

[8]   The established name of the wall is 'Feldsteinmauer' in Germany and 'kampestensmuren' in Denmark (see also Table 1). In English a direct translation would be 'Fieldstone Wall' which is used in this text, which does, though, not necessarily mean that all the stones were collected in the surrounding fields.

[9]   This is not always the case: only about 30 m to the east the Fieldstone Wall sits a few metres in front (south) of the older ditch (Kramer 1984: 345 Abb. 2), proving a – at least partly – different alignment of both.

Figure 8: The Fieldstone Wall west of the gate as seen from the north-west. Here the stone wall is comparatively poorly preserved, as it was used as a quarry to gain stones for the foundation of the Waldemarsmauer (also see Figure 10)

Figure 9: The section of the Main Rampart of the Danevirke and the back of the Fieldstone Wall as seen from the north. The height of the remains of the ramparts plus Fieldstone Wall is almost 4m

later was followed by and incorporated in the Fieldstone Wall. One of the main reasons to believe this is that the characteristic posts of the Palisade occur not only where the Fieldstone Wall was extant, but also where it was never built (e.g. in the North and East Ramparts and in parts of the Main Rampart, too see Figure 2 and 5). However, the evidence also suggests (in contrast to Andersen's view) that the Palisade (phase 4 of the Main Rampart see Figure 5) was not contemporary with the Turf Wall (phase 3 of the Main Rampart see Figure 5) but represents either a much later addition to it or a renewal of its derelict front.

Although the Fieldstone Wall was not excavated, in order to properly preserve the remains, the medieval disturbances in the wall were used (Figure 10) to get an (almost) non-destructive look at details of its construction. In at least three different locations it became clear that the lower rows of stones did not quite fit into the direction of the stone body on top. In some places the stones stuck out, whereas in others they were clearly set back from the stones above. Additionally, the lower stones had not been dressed, as was the case with many of the stones on top, and the mortar the stones were set in was clearly different: in the upstanding wall it was a yellow clay whereas, it was grey clay between the stones beneath. Scientific analysis carried out by Kaare Lund Rasmussen of Syddansk Universitet, Odense showed a clear difference between the two types of clay, caused by the different origins of the material. This evidence suggests that there might have been two building phases for the Fieldstone Wall (Rasmussen 2013: 188ff).

Remains of a comparable single layer of stones were found in 1971 by Andersen and Madsen while excavating the North Rampart, which has the row of substantial post as described above, but no Fieldstone Wall (Andersen 1998: 101, figure 106 and 107). Additionally, during his excavation at the North Rampart in 1933, Herbert Jankuhn found stones in a similar position which he described as 'of unknown purpose' (Jankuhn 1937: 168).

There is, therefore, some evidence (posts and stone layer under the Fieldstone Wall and in other parts of the Danevirke such as the North Rampart) which indicates that an independent building Phase 4 (Palisade) existed and preceded Phase 5 (Fieldstone Wall) (see Figure 5 Main Rampart).

Mainly, but not solely, based on these observations, there is more and more reason to doubt that the Fieldstone Wall was actually built in or around AD 740 and it is more plausible that it was added a few decades later, as suggested by Andersen (Andersen 1998: 183) and that it may even be associated with the Danevirke of King Godfred mentioned in the Royal Frankish Annals from the early ninth century (Scholz 1972).[10]

While the precise dating might be disputed, the excavated evidence provides strong

---

[10] Regarding the reinforcement of the Danevirke by King Godfred recorded in the Royal Frankish Annals Dobat (2008:41) concludes a renovation of older structures. On the background of the latest observations, it is now possible, that the Fieldstone Wall might be the missing 'Godfred's Danevirke'.

Figure 10: The Fieldstone Wall west of the gate looking west. In the centre, the photo shows oval disturbances (white arrows) in the Fieldstone Wall, where stones were taken away to build the foundation of the brick wall (grey rectangle)

evidence that the Danevirke was reinforced heavily during the eighth century, including the construction of a massive 4km-long Fieldstone Wall. These substantial extensions are a clear and early indicator of a strong ruler north of the Danevirke marking the border of his territory, not only creating a physical obstacle to keep out unwanted visitors, but also demonstrating his ability and authority to have a wall of monumental size and strength built.

The (Viking Age) gateway

In 2010, it had become clear that there was a 5 or 6m-wide gap in the Fieldstone Wall (Figure 3). After the removal of the thirteenth century fill a 3.5m-wide sandy trackway was found, which proved to be the remains of one of many layers of a road which must have run through the Danevirke since the gate was established (Figure 11).

It consists of thin layers of eroded sand, which show marks of cart tracks (Schovsbo 2013: 206). These layers are remains of a sunken road, and a deposit of charcoal on top of these sediments, which has provided a couple of radiocarbon dates to the second half of the tenth century (Tummuscheit and Witte 2013: 17–18).

At present, it is clear that this passage through the Danevirke had been in use since at least the erection of the Turf Wall (see above and Figure 7), perhaps even since the very first earthen rampart and that it ceased to be used some time during the thirteenth century. The passage was therefore open for at least 700 years – probably more – and had cut itself deep into the glacial sand forming a hollow way. The lowest surface of this sunken road lay more than 1m below the base of the Fieldstone Wall.

The discovery of the gate and the entrance way through the rampart showed, for the first time, the existence of a central gate in the Main Rampart, which was established at the same time as the second main building phase (Turf Wall), it is possible even at the same time as the first phase. Before this discovery, Danevirke gates were only known from the tenth and eleventh century (Dobat 2008: 57–58).

The Medieval Rampart (Phase 6)

In 2010, the starting point of the twelfth-century brick wall, the Waldemarsmauer (Phase 6 of the Main Rampart see Figure 5), was identified, although only a tiny bit of this mighty brick wall had survived within the limits of our excavation. From the foundation of the Waldemarsmauer, we could define to the nearest centimetre the point where the construction of the wall was begun in the late twelfth century (Figure 10). This point lies about 10 m to the west of the newly found gateway. On the eastern side of the gate there were no traces of the Brick Wall whatsoever (Witte and Tummuscheit 2018: 73).

The medieval road

The area south of the Danevirke gate which has ditches and remains of several road surfaces was also excavated (Figure 12). There were both sandy layers and layers of cobblestones, which might represent remains of road surfaces, but the post-excavation work is still ongoing. All these features run parallel with the rampart on the eastern side of the gate and head into the direction of the gate, although they are not preserved there. Connected to what is probably the newest phase of pathways, remains of more than 30 wooden posts, which were dendro-chronologically dated to around AD 1200, were found. Additionally, a sherd of highly decorated earthenware, pieces of a wooden drinking cup, building stones of imported tufa[11] and other finds from the same period show that the gate was not closed by that time (of the death of Waldemar I in 1182), and the rampart and road were not only still in use, but also have been subject to extension and rebuilding (Witte and Tummuscheit 2018: 73).

Defence and a show of force

Through its lifetime, the Danevirke consistently served as a physical barrier to the movement of people, resources and materials – and it still remains the largest scheduled monument in Northern Europe (Northern Germany and Scandinavia). It was certainly built as a means to protect an area, to draw a line, which would assist any defensive measures. In between the different phases of building activities, archaeological evidence shows times of

---

[11] Building material made of rock composed of volcanic detritus, fused together by heat imported from the Eifel-area south-west of Cologne. The building stones were used for the construction of churches mainly on the southern and western coasts of the North Sea but also in the Schleswig area.

Figure 11: The remains of one of many roads, which has survived as a 3.5m-wide sandy trackway looking north-east

non-use for shorter and longer periods until a new defence was raised, often built in front of its predeceasing structure.

The early earthen ramparts, the Fieldstone Wall and the Brick Wall – which always face to the south – could be seen from a distance and surely made an impression on the populations living within its environs, both friends and foes. Besides controlling movement, protecting trade routes and being a major military stronghold the Danevirke would have functioned as a symbol and a political statement the power of the state that built it too.

The erection of the Fieldstone Wall and the Brick Wall elevated the rampart to new heights. Not only in regard to the building techniques adopted, which were state of the art in their respective times, but also concerning their enhanced visual impact, the Danevirke was not just a barrier but a symbol of elite, perhaps royal, power.

In the eighth century, the massive 4km-long and 3m-high Fieldstone Wall had no equivalent in the whole of Northern Europe. Certainly, other ramparts (like hillforts) were ditched earthworks with sometimes possible additional built wooden palisades. Yet, no other stone constructions of a comparable size are known from the area until around the twelfth century. The scale of each stage of building work was unprecedented.

Figure 12: The area south of the Danevirke gate during the excavation in 2014 looking southwest. The fills of ditches and remains of trackways are visible. The stones in the forefront are remains of a slope below the rampart east of the gate which was covered with a layer of clay with stones on top. On the western side of the gate the same feature appears

Indeed, it is probable that the stones used for the Fieldstone Wall were not gathered locally but more likely transported from the east coast, which was 30km away.[12] As a result of this project, it is estimated that some twenty million stones were transported: this was an enormous undertaking and a highly skilled and well-organised workforce would be needed to build with the new material.

This use of new construction material on the Danevirke was repeated in 1162/3 when Waldermar I 'The Great' built the Brick Wall. This is a time when bricks as building material were still largely unknown in Northern Europe. It is therefore presumed that the labour to build a 4km-long and up to 5m (7m if topped by a wooden palisade) high wall, would have had to be imported from Italy and France, in order to have the necessarily skill base to construct one of the earliest (and definitely the largest) brick built structure in the whole of Northern Europe.

Who were its builders then? For the medieval Brick Wall we know it was Waldemar I (Schindel 1999: 65-66). Moving back to the late Viking Age, the tenth-century activities can be attributed to Harald Bluetooth (Dobat 2005: 148). For the early Viking age, the

---

[12] See also footnote 7.

written sources hint at King Godfred (Scholz 1972; Tummuscheit and Witte 2018: 76). Yet for the very beginning in the late Iron Age, the written sources are very rare and there is not yet sufficiently evidence enough to give an answer. Presumably there must have been a central leader or a group of rulers powerful enough to claim the area for themselves and with enough authority to get a population of people to undertake the construction work.

In any case, it is the first time the limits of the southern extent of the area which would later be known as Denmark were defined. This would have been a monumental structure, which even in times that there was no need for any fortification on that boundary, the rampart stood, marking the border of the emerging state. The longevity of the Danevirke can be exemplified that it was in such good condition that it was even reused as a military defense in both 1864 and 1944 (Andersen 2004: 81–85; Kühl and Hardt 1999: 93–124, 139–44).

The context and comparator monuments

With its sequence of several major building phases, the usage of different materials and times of abandonment and reuse for about seven hundred years the Danevirke stands alone compared to other linear earthworks in Europe. Linear earthworks first appear in the first and second centuries in Jutland which typically consists of banks and palisades with ditches of modest size, mostly used as road blockers (Spring 2015: 117).

Later on, a wide range of types of fortification were used in Scandinavia. The different types and building materials reflect the local topography and resources. Most of them are poorly understood or even not investigated at all, therefore details of their building history and precise dating are often unknown. In the mid-/late first millennium AD, we have evidence of sea barriers, hillforts and fortified refuges, urban town banks, and during the early second millennium AD we have castles and town walls. Yet despite this variability, the Danevirke stands alone: there is no other linear earthwork of the Viking Age or the Middle Ages (Spring 2015: 109–17). The closest comparison comes from the ramparts of tenth-century at Birka in Sweden, which are earthen banks with ditches and a timbered palisade (Roesdahl 1993: 210). The Birka system actually relates to the semicircular rampart at Hedeby – which is one part of the whole Danevirke system itself. Additionally, a 2km-long stone wall named Tunborg – probably from the Viking Age – is known from the Swedish island of Gotland where an older fortified refuge was extended (Roesdahl 1993: 210, figure 24).

During the reign of King Waldemar I of Denmark in the twelfth century, at the same time as the Brick Wall was added to the Danevirke, only a few castles and the church of Ringsted (1161) were built using brick. In Norway and Sweden castles and churches of the Middle Ages were built of stone almost exclusively.

In Germany, earthworks of the Roman Iron Age were described by Tacitus (Dorey 1969; Gudeman 1900). These were built in order to control and defend Roman territory against the 'barbarians', the Roman Limes were built from the first century AD. The extent of these earthworks are around 550 km long, including all building phases such as roads, earthen banks, ditches and palisades. In around AD 206/207, at the Upper Germanic-Rhaetian Limes (Raetischer Limes), an earthen bank and ditch were converted into a stone wall up to 3m high, known as the 'Teufelsmauer' (Devils Wall) (Nunn 2009: 93–97).

Britain has many linear earthworks or dykes mostly made of an earthen bank with a ditch (Bell 2012). They date from the Bronze Age to the early medieval period. In the Roman period, Hadrian's Wall (built from AD 122) was originally built from turf like the second oldest main phase of the Danevirke (Phase 3 of the Main Rampart; see Figure 5), and then later a shell wall of stone was constructed (Bell 2012: 95-97). It is possible that's its forerunner probably was the stone wall 'Teufelsmauer', a part of the Limes. Like Hadrian's Wall and the Danevirkes Fieldstone Wall the 'Teufelsmauer' was constructed as a shell wall.

Regarding Offa's Dyke, both monuments share a lot of similarities; reputedly they both stretch from sea to sea and were developed in several stages. Both the Danevirke and Offa's Dyke have been dated to originate from the eighth century AD, but as discussed above, recent investigations now have radiocarbon dates from the fifth century AD for the Turf Wall of the Danevirke. Similarly, radiocarbon analysis was being undertaken on the bank of Offa's Dyke and showed the possibility for it to have been built sometime after AD 430, tentatively suggesting an earlier date of construction than previously believed (Belford 2017: 69). Additionally, the function and role of the two ramparts as physical barriers serving as territorial markers and as symbols of power are comparable, as are the functions of control of populations and military expansion alternating with phases of abandonment. The central part of the Danevirke was built in a straight line with gateways and roads and Offa's Dyke is postulated to be of a similar design. Further, both the Danevirke and Offa's Dyke were built to be monumental displays to be seen from a long distance and designed to lead existing roads to gates to control access (Belford 2017: 62–83).

Conclusion

Some of the results presented in this article remain in the preliminary stages and are subject of an ongoing research project. It is, however, already certain that the new excavations have led to new results with far-reaching consequences, especially concerning the dating of the earliest and the latest phases of the Danevirke, which have already fundamentally changed the view of the Danevirke and its complex biography from at least the fifth century to the present day.

Bibliography

Andersen, H.H. 1985. Zum neuen Schnitt am Hauptwall des Danewerks. *Archäologisches Korrespondenzblatt* 15: 525–529.

Andersen, H.H. 1998. *Danevirke og Kovirke. Arkæologiske undersøgelser 1861–1993.* Århus: Aarhus Universitetsforlag.

Andersen, H.H. 2004. *Til hele rigets værn. Danevirkes arkæologi og historie.* Højbjerg: Moesgard og Wormianum.

Becker-Christensen, H. 1981. *Hærvejen i Sønderjylland – et vejhistorisk studie. Fra Kongeåen til Danevirke.* Apenrade: Institut for Grænseregionsforskning.

Belford, P. 2017. Offa's Dyke: a line in the landscape, in T. Jenkins and R. Abbiss (eds) *Fortress Salopia.* Solihull: Heliaon: 60–81.

Bell, M. 2012. *The Archaeology of the Dykes. From the Romans to Offa`s Dyke.* Stroud: Amberley.

Dobat, A.S. 2005. Danevirke – a linear earthwork in the province of Schleswig and Holstein and its socio-political background, in M. Segschneider (ed.) *Ringwälle und verwandte Strukturen des ersten Jahrtausends n. Chr. an Nord- und Ostsee.* Neumünster: Wachholtz Verlag: 137–157.

Dobat, A.S. 2008. Danevirke Revisited: An Investigation into Military and Socio-political Organization in South Scandinavia (c AD 700 to 1100). *Mediaeval Archaeology 52:* 27–67.

Dorey, T.A. 1969. 'Agricola' and 'Germania' in, T. A. Dorey (ed. and trans.) *Tacitus:* 1–18. London: Routledge.

Ethelberg, P. 2012. Den tidlige rigsdannelse i Slesvig (AD 150-450), in L. N. Henningsen, L. S. Madsen, O. Madsen (eds) *Det Sønderjyske Landbrugs historie. Jernalder, vikingetid og middelalder.* Haderslev: Museum Sønderjylland – Arkæologi Haderslev og Historisk Samfund for Sønderjylland: 272–300.

Ethelberg, P. 2017. Anglerriget storhed og fald. *Skalk* 2017 3: 15–27.

Gudeman, A. 1900. The Sources of the Germania of Tacitus. *Transactions and Proceedings of the American Philological Association* 31: 93–111.

Hamann, G.F. 1861. Danevirke (unpublished report National Museum Kopenhagen).

Harck, O. 1998. Anmerkungen zum Primärwall des Danewerkes, in A. Wesse (ed.) *Studien zur Archäologie des Ostseeraums. Festschrift für Michael Müller-Wille.* Neumünster: Wachholtz Verlag: : 127–134.

Haseloff, G. 1937. Die Ausgrabungen am Danewerk und ihre Ergebnisse. *Offa* 2: 111–167.

Holst, M.K. 2013. The construction of Skelhøj: Introduction, in M.K. Holst and M. Rasmussen (eds) *Skelhøj and the Bronze Age Barrows of Southern Scandinavia: Vol. I. The Bronze Age barrow tradition and the excavation of Skelhøj.* Jysk Arkæologisk Selskab, Højbjerg, Jysk Arkæologisk Selskabs Skrifter, vol. 78.

Jankuhn, H. 1937. *Die Wehranlagen der Wikingerzeit zwischen Schlei und Treene* (Ausgrabungen in Haithabu 1). Neumünster: Karl Wachholz Verlag.

Jankuhn, H. 1986. *Haithabu. Ein Handelsplatz der Wikingerzeit*. 8th edition. Neumünster: Wachholtz Verlag.

Jensen J. 2006. *Danmarks Oldtid. Yngre jernalder og vikingetid 400–1050 e.Kr.* Gyldendal: Viborg.

Kramer, W. 1984. Die Datierung der Feldsteinmauer des Danewerks – Vorbericht einer neuen Ausgrabung am Hauptwall. *Archäologisches Korrespondenzblatt* 14: 343–350.

Kramer, W. 1992. Ein hölzernes Sperrwerk in der Großen Breite der Schlei als Teil des Danewerk-Baues von 737 n. Chr. Geb. *Archäologische Nachrichten aus Schleswig-Holstein* 3: 82–96.

Kramer, W. 1995. Das Seesperrwerk bei Reesholm in der Schlei. *Archäologische Nachrichten aus Schleswig-Holstein* 6: 42–53.

Kühl J. and Hardt N. 1999. *Danevirke. Nordens største fortidsminde.* Herning: Poul Kristensens Forlag.

La Cour, V. 1951. *Danevirkestudier. En arkæologisk-historisk undersøgelse.* København: P. Haase and Søns Forlag.

Madsen L.S. 2018. Hærvejen. *Sønderjysk Månedsskrift* 3: 83–89.

Madsen, O. 2008. Forhistorien indtil 700, in H. Schultz Hansen, L. N. Henningsen and C. Porskrog Rasmussen (eds) *Sønderjyllands historie* 1. Aabenraa: Historisk Samfund for Sønderjylland : 11–40.

Maluck, M. A. 2017. Reviewing the functions of the Danevirke, in B. Valentin Eriksen, A. Abegg-Wigg, R. Bleile and U. Ickerodt (eds) *Interaktion ohne Grenzen. Beispiele archäologischer Forschungen am Beginn des 21. Jahrhunderts.* Schleswig 2017: 607–618.

Maluck, M. and Weltecke, Chr. (ed.). 2016. The Archaeological Border Landscape of Hedeby and Danevirke. A German nomination to UNESCO's World Heritage List (unpublished application).

Müller, S. and C. Neergaard. 1903. *Danevirke. Archæologisk undersøgt, beskrevet og tydet.* Offprint of Vol. 1 of Nordiske fortidsminder. København, Kongelige Nordiske Oldskriftselskab.

Nunn, A. 2009. *Mauern als Grenzen.* Mainz: Verlag Philipp von Zabern.

Rasmussen, K. Lund. 2013. *Dannevirke-1. Data and interpretations.* Unpublished report.

Roesdahl, E. 1993. *Fortification*, in Philip Pulsiano (ed) *Mediaeval Scandinavia: An Encyclopedia*: 209-216. New York and London: Garland Publishing Inc.

Schindel, S. 1999. *Die Backsteinmauer im Danewerk.* Schriftliche Hausarbeit zur Erlangung des Grades eines Magister Artium (M.A.) der Philosophischen Fakultät der Christian-Albrechts-Universität zu Kiel. Kiel 1999.

Schovsbo, P.O. 2013. Besigtigelse 8. Oktober 2013 Dannevirke Kr. SF LA 85. Unpublished report.

Scholz, B.W. (trans.) 1972. *Carolingian chronicles: Royal Frankish Annals and Nithard's Histories*, Ann Arbor: University of Michigan Press.

Spring, P. 2015. *Great Walls and Linear Barriers.* South Yorkshire: Pen and Sword.

Tummuscheit, A. 2011. Das neu entdeckte Tor im Danewerk – Einer der geschichtsträchtigsten Orte Schleswig-Holsteins. *Archäologische Nachrichten aus Schleswig-Holstein* 17: 84-87. Neumünster/Hamburg: Wachholtz Verlag.

Tummuscheit, A. and Witte, F. 2013. Bericht über die Ausgrabung 2013 in Dannewerk LA 85, Kr. Schleswig-Flensburg. Unpublished report.

Tummuscheit, A. and Witte, F. 2014a. Bericht über die Ausgrabung 2014 in Dannewerk LA 85, Kr. Schleswig-Flensburg. Unpublished report.

Tummuscheit, A. and Witte, F. 2014b. Der einzige Weg durchs Danewerk. Zu den Ausgrabungen am Danewerk im Jahr 2013. *Archäologie in Schleswig/Arkæologi i Slesvig* 15: 153–162.

Witte, F. 2017. Porten i Danevirke. *Skalk* 2017 no. 1: 3–9.

Witte F. and Tummuscheit, A. 2018. The Danevirke in the light of the recent excavations, in J. Hansen and M. Bruuns (eds) *The Fortified Viking Age.* Odense: University Press of Southern Denmark: 69–74.

Astrid Tummuscheit, Archäologisches Landesamt Schleswig-Holstein, Brockdorff-Rantzau-Str. 70, 24837 Schleswig, Germany
        Email: astrid.tummuscheit@alsh.landsh.de

Frauke Witte, Museum Sønderjylland, Viden & Samlinger, Arkæologi, Dalgade 7, Dk-6100 – Haderslev, Denmark
        Email: frwi@msj.dk

Making Earthworks Visible: The Example of the Oswestry Heritage Comics Project

John Swogger

The example of the Oswestry Heritage Comics *Project demonstrates how the use of informational comics can raise awareness of heritage which, though highly visible, can be readily overlooked. This has particular implications for linear earthwork monuments which vary in their surviving monumentality and accessibility, including Offa's Dyke and Wat's Dyke, where poor public understanding can contribute to their vulnerability. Comics have the potential to make these monuments better understood, and thus more visible to – and potentially more valued by – the communities which live alongside them.*

Keywords: borders, art, comics, heritage, Oswestry, Shropshire, Wat's Dyke

As an archaeologist and an archaeological illustrator with over twenty-five years' experience in the field, outreach is an essential component of my work. As an illustrator, it is essential I make sure that the drawings and paintings I produce explain sites effectively; from an archaeological perspective it is important that good explanations of archaeological evidence help to build meaningful relationships with research colleagues, community stakeholders, official bodies and funders, all of which can impact public involvement with research, but also access to sites, project logistics, budgets and research outcomes.

Nevertheless, specialist archaeological visualisation methods, such as finds illustration and even some reconstructions, can require considerable explanation and interpretation in order to 'make sense' to non-specialist audiences. Informational comics are capable of communicating research about the past in an effective and engaging way to public and specialist audiences alike (Atalay 2012: 192). This in part is due to the fact that comics allow for the close and integrated use of both text and image within a single composition. In informational comics, visual context and text-based explanation are combined, meaning the specific qualities and strengths of each can be exercised, as well as reinforced by the qualities and strengths of the other (Swogger 2000: 148). This combination approach creates a composition which informs on multiple levels: both visual and semantic, left-brain and right-brain, passive and active (Shanks 1997: 78). This, in turn, reinforces readers' connections to the material under discussion, and can improve rates both of comprehension and retention (Hosler and Boomer 2011). In this article, I explore the specific potential for informational comics in engaging communities with the heritage of borderlands, of which linear earthworks and other natural and human-made frontiers are an integral part, focusing on the *Oswestry Heritage Comics.*

Offa's Dyke Journal volume 1 2019
Manuscript received: 29 May 2019
accepted: 10 September 2019

Figure 1: Two strips from the Oswestry Heritage Comics series – (a) *Bringing Heritage to Life* (Swogger 2019a: 7), (b) *Oswestry Castle Exvations* (Swogger 2019a: 13)

Comics and archaeological information: the *Oswestry Heritage Comics* project

Between 2016 and 2018, I wrote and illustrated two separate series of comics about the archaeology, history and heritage of the Anglo-Welsh borderlands market town of Oswestry (Shropshire). Funded by the Heritage Lottery Fund (HLF 2017), *Oswestry Heritage Comics*[1] were published weekly over eighteen months in the *Oswestry & Border Counties Advertizer* newspaper, as well as online on Facebook, on the website of Oswestry Community Arts, and on the author's own Wordpress blog (Figures 1 and 2).[2]

---

[1]   https://johngswogger.wordpress.com/tag/oswestry-heritage-comics/page/2/. 'Oswestry Heritage Comics' was the title of the HLF-funded project. 'Oswestry Heritage' was also the main title to each strip referred to here collectively as the 'Oswestry Heritage' comics. The title of the anthology (to which all references refer) was 'The Oswestry Heritage Comics'.

[2]   The first series of the comics ran in the Advertizer June–September 2016, and the second series June 2017–June 2018. There was a series of A5 poster-versions of the comics posted between September 2016–June 2017 (some of these are still up in Oswestry Library at the time of writing (June 2019).

Figure 2: Two strips from the Oswestry Heritage Comics series (a) The Llwyd Eagle (Swogger 2019a: 14), (b) Learning From the Past (Swogger 2019a: 19).

Through both digital and physical dissemination, the comics became highly visible within the community of Oswestry and its environs, and, judging from comments from readers both online and, in person, often whilst writing and drawing the comic in town, caught the attention of people who otherwise would not necessarily visit museums or have any other involvement with their local heritage (Swogger 2019a: 23).

The comics were able to introduce a wide range of heritage subjects to their audience: ranging from prehistory to the Napoleonic war, covering themes from transport to family history, and both current archaeological excavations as well as new research by local historians. Their short format and condensed style meant that they could quite happily shift temporal and thematic focus from comic to comic, or even panel to panel. This allowed each subject to be placed within an historical context, and also demonstrated how local heritage is not confined to a single time, or place. The *Oswestry Heritage Comics* aimed to present geology, industry and tourism, ecology, archaeology and social history as equal components of our local past.

Importantly, covering a broad range of heritage, in conjunction with a focus on *who* is interested in these subjects, means that local heritage can be made relevant through the interest and involvement of local enthusiasts and researchers. This then allows the discussion of how that interest and involvement makes heritage visible and relevant for others (Swogger 2019a: 12, 13, 34, 40). The comics have also been an excellent way to highlight the work of local community-based heritage organisations. In Oswestry there is, for example, the Oswestry & Border History and Archaeology Group, an active organisation since the excavations at Rhyn Park Roman marching camp in 1977 (Swogger 2019a: 5). The comics are able to support their investigations on the historic environment by signposting their work, as well as shining a light upon the ongoing challenges that each faces with regards conservation and awareness (Swogger 2019a: 48, 50).

The aesthetic, style and a narrative context of comics can also effectively convey unfamiliar concepts through the use of a decluttered explanatory structure. The layered relationship between image and text within comics allows for plenty of complexity within the content. Even a diversity of new information - archaeology, history, rambling, footpaths, folklore and community stewardship - can be combined in such a way that, even within a small space, feels both natural and complementary (Swogger 2019a: 78, 11).

Establishing this connection between site/monument/place and people then allows one to explore different kinds local engagement with heritage. Once this connection is made, it also provides a basis for exploring scholarly interest in the local past, and to demonstrate the national and international context for other local research projects, whether community based, or lead by professional scholars (Swogger 2019a: 19, 34, 42).

Having introduced the idea that there are many ways to engage with information about local history, heritage and archaeology, the comic can then help demonstrate how there is heritage all around us, hidden in plain sight; revealing the unexpected and the extraordinary that can be found in our everyday landscapes and places. This embedding of heritage and heritage research within the community then invites discussion of what the past means to us in the present: how heritage can be more than just dates and names of kings, but how it can be about the ordinary and the everyday. In this context, such discussions inevitably raise questions of how heritage will be safeguarded for future generations, and prompt suggestions for how 'non-specialists' can get involved in local heritage (Swogger 2019a: 44, 48, 50).

Comics can produce these results by employing two different key mechanisms. First, by combining text and image, they reinvent the idea of 'show and tell'. In a comic, visual context and narrative explanation are not just close at hand, or side-by-side, they are interdependent and inter-related. Each does what it does best, but each does so as part of a 'team effort' (McCloud 2006: 128 ff.) (Figures 3 and 4).

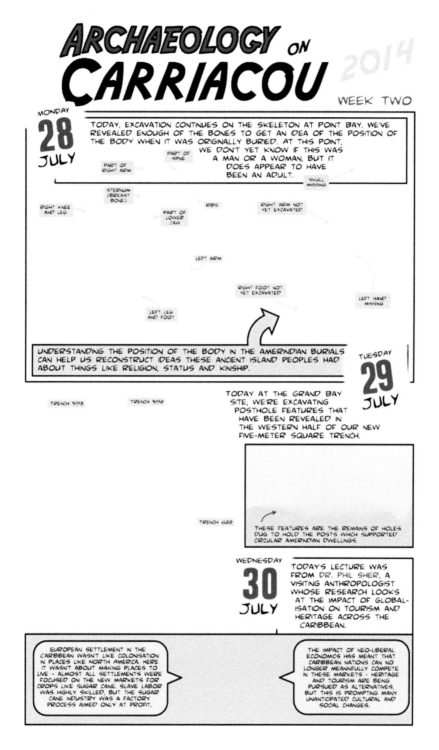

Figure 3: An 'excavated' page from a comic to show the text without the images, from *Archaeology on Carriacou 2014*, University of Oregon/University College London. Poster in Hillsborough, Carriaciou, 2014

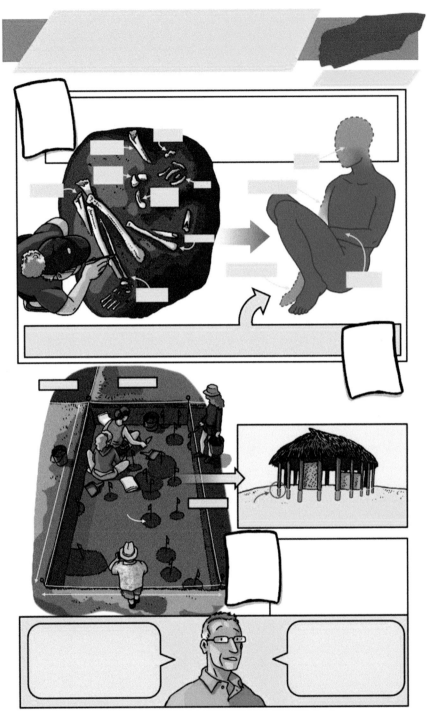

Figure 4: An 'excavated' page from a comic to show the images without the text. Together with Figure 3 it shows the different kinds of information conveyed by image and text. *Archaeology on Carriacou 2014,* University of Oregon/University College London. Poster in Hillsborough, Carriaciou, 2014

Second, this multi-layered approach to presenting text and image together allows an informational comic to both serve as an introduction and a reminder. Familiar images reinforce unfamiliar knowledge, while unfamiliar images invite the reader to revisit known facts. This multi-layered approach to information which serves to show and tell, introduce and remind, means that audiences do not necessarily have to come to the comic with any prior knowledge. It de-complicates without dumbing down; simplifies without making simplistic. Importantly, is not a reductive mechanism, but an additive one: individual elements such as captions, pictures, speech-balloons and panels are pieced together by the reader one by one. As a result, learning might occur as a literal step-by-step process, which means that readers are actively engaged in constructing their own knowledge of the subject (an explicit example of this being the US Army engineering/maintenance comics of Will Eisner: Campbell 2011; see also McCloud 1993:60 ff., 2006: 14 ff.).

This approach ensures that comics are both accessible and engaging. In the case of the *Oswestry Heritage Comics*, this has resulted in them being widely read and broadly shared. Their publication in the local newspaper meant that they were seen by eighteen thousand people every week in print, reaching approximately 40% of households in Oswestry itself. Each comic was also read by an average of three thousand Facebook readers online, who had shared and re-posted the comic via blogs and social media for an even wider distribution. Establishing formal metrics for the impact of comics can be problematic, since they are often used to communicate with audiences in spaces where collecting feedback becomes difficult. However, a recent online survey for the *Oswestry Heritage Comics* project suggested respondents (n = 1% of Facebook readers) found the comic not only entertaining and informative, but easier to process than text-based outreach and more likely to prompt onward engagement with heritage. Indeed, over a third of the survey respondents indicated that they had become more actively involved in heritage as a result of reading the comics. While these results could not measure specific impacts on comprehension and information retention, they do at least chime well with other studies into the effectiveness of comics both as a way of imparting information, and as a way of changing attitudes among readers (cf. Hostler and Boomer 2011, McNicol 2017, Swogger 2019a: 24).

However, such quantitative measures are – in this case – imprecise tools. They provide a snapshot only, and do not adequately give a picture of broader and longer-term impacts; understanding the legacy of an outreach project is at least as important as understanding its immediate reception. In the case of the *Oswestry Heritage Comics*, qualitative, anecdotal measures of impact have provided me with a much more complete understanding of the value of the project and of comics as a communication medium for heritage. Such feedback can be difficult to record, however. Chance conversations in pubs and coffee shops gave me a real sense of what people actually thought about the comics and how enhanced their appreciation for or interest in local archaeology and history, but such conversations generally pass by unrecorded – except, perhaps, when they happen during a radio interview:

I knew a bit about Saint Oswald – but I've learnt more in four pictures and a bit of writing – you've made me read that. I've actually read *that*, as opposed to it being in a long [newspaper] column... You could see people *actually* reading that – young and old, and it's gone in... It's amazing. It's very, very good.

Eric Smith, BBC Radio Shropshire, 8 September 2017 (BBC 2017)

A more concrete form of feedback is to look at what a project like the *Oswestry Heritage Comics* leads to: in other words, whether other local heritage organisations also start to regard comics as an effective and engaging form of outreach for their own projects. Since June 2018, when the *Oswestry Heritage Comics* finished in the Oswestry Advertizer, I have been commissioned for three new local comics projects. The first was a two-part, half-page comic about a First World War heritage project run by Qube called 'Homefront Heroines' (Swogger 2019c), looking at the roles of local women during wartime. The second is a series of twelve full-page informational and outreach comics in the Oswestry Advertizer as part of the 'Old Oswestry Discovery Project', a Heritage Lottery Funded project. The third, in production during 2019–2020, is an informational comic book about the life of King – later Saint – Oswald, who gave his name to the town of Oswestry, to be distributed during the 2020 Saint Oswald's Festival in town. Beyond Oswestry, the four-panel heritage comic model developed during the *Oswestry Heritage Comics* project was explicitly referenced by clients for two non-UK based comics projects. Firstly, by the Heritage Research Group Caribbean when they commissioned in 2018 a series of ten four-panel comics about the heritage of Grenada, and secondly by a British Council project commissioned for 2020 for comics about heritage on the island of Soqotra, off the coast of Yemen. All this suggests a high degree of confidence among clients as to the effectiveness of comics as a communications medium for history, archaeology and heritage. In particular, the organiser of the Saint Oswald's Festival – an event which is being backed by the Town Council and the Rotary Club – explicitly cited the 'around town' reception of the comic about St. Oswald from the *Oswestry Heritage Comics* series (Swogger 2019a: 11) in commissioning the comic book biography, and is using the *Oswestry Heritage Comics* strip in advance publicity for the festival at this year's Heritage Open Days.

Additionally, interest among local heritage groups in hearing more about the use of comics as outreach has remained consistently high. Between 2016 and summer 2019 I was invited to give more than a dozen talks on the *Oswestry Heritage Comics* and related comics projects to WI groups, library learning clubs, local and not-so-local museum and archaeology societies (travelling as far as Stoke-on-Trent to do so), as well as presenting papers about the project at archaeology conferences (TAG, the Society for American Archaeology and the American Anthropological Association), comics conferences (Comics Forum UK, the Applied Comics Network), and even being invited as a guest panellist to San Diego Comic Fest in 2018 and the much larger San Diego Comic Con in 2019 to talk about comics and community heritage.

Though the above is difficult to quantify, onward projects clearly based in an evaluation of the impact of the *Oswestry Heritage Comics*, and continuing interest from the broader heritage community demonstrate that both groups feel comics are of interest and of value in communicating local heritage. Indeed, a direct example of this makes its way into one of the *Oswestry Heritage Comics* strips (Swogger 2019a: 23). Mark and Rachel were typical of the kind of people who read the comic but were unlikely to complete an online survey or a questionnaire handout. They found the comics engaging and interesting – enough so that when they found an unusual carved stone in their garden, they approached me for more information about it, and were delighted when I asked if their story could be turned into one of the comics in the series. Mark and Rachel's engagement illustrates very well the sort of appeal, interest and value the comics have inspired – and does so, in my opinion, far better than any quantitative metrics. Indeed, it may be the case that anecdote is the only way to effectively measure and understand the impact of such comics.

Comics and earthwork monuments

Earthwork monuments can sometimes be difficult to understand. At least with a ruined castle or other stone construction identifiable architectural components such as wall-faces, turrets, windows, doors, and steps survive which audiences can imagine being used by people in the past. Earthworks can often become eroded, dismantled, forgotten or even erased; the borders and frontiers they relate to those of vanished people and polities, or transient cultural and political distinctions. Offa's Dyke is at once on the border between England and Wales (Hay-on-Wye to Monmouth), then in England (as at Oswestry) and then in Wales (as at Llangollen) at different points along its length, making talking about it as a 'frontier' complex. Even when an earthwork like Offa's Dyke survives, it can be difficult to see precisely because of the larger-than-human scale, becoming overlain by vegetation and obscured by other land-uses. Overcoming this lack of visibility and contemporary resonance presents a challenge to those visualising such monuments. We may be familiar with earthworks as flood defences or landscaping, but we are not necessarily familiar with them as military monuments or as frontier markers. A reconstruction drawing of an earthen bank and ditch may give little clue as to its true impact at the time of construction.

The way comics present information may be able to give earthwork monuments a different kind of visibility and significance by presenting the monument alongside its changing (or changed) cultural or temporal context. Readers of a comic might be able to find something familiar in the monument not based on how it once looked, but through being shown how it was originally made and used – or, indeed, how it is used (or mis-used) today. Outreach about earthwork monuments like Offa's and Wat's Dyke, can show the ancient monument and its original function while at the same time discussing contemporary meaning and place, inviting people to get involved, understanding how heritage can be 'hidden in plain sight', and emphasising the collective contribution of local researchers, community groups and heritage professionals. The panel-by-panel structure of comics can then be used to layer this diverse information within a sequential narrative, perhaps based around the monument's construction.

Figure 5 is an equivalent to the phase drawings or plans used in archaeology all the time, but the comic embeds the missing narrative element, interrelating the necessary 'other half' of the story and making the sequence accessible for non-specialists. A visual rebuilding of Offa's Dyke by process, through time, framed by a narrative explanation, situated in an inhabited historical context might enable those unfamiliar with both earthwork construction in general and the dyke in particular to 'see' it; and having 'seen' it as a thing in the past, to understand its current state in the present.

Given the damage already suffered by earthwork monuments through ignorance and oversight, presenting outreach like this in local newspapers and local online communities becomes particularly important. The *Oswestry Heritage Comics* series featured short comics about both Offa's and Wat's Dyke and offers an example of the way different kinds of information can be effectively presented within even the relatively small amount of space available in a local weekly paper.

The Wat's Dyke comic started by explaining the possible origins of the earthwork's name, featured a panel briefly considering the construction of the dyke, then looked at both its past and present context (Figure 6). The level of information was kept relatively general, as it was discovered prior to writing the comic that many local readers had never heard of the monument, and those that did principally wanted to know why it was called 'Wat's' Dyke. Here again, 'showing and telling' allows the comic to provide a visual context for an explanation about the monument's name, purpose and origins. It both introduces readers to the possibly unfamiliar past, and, through its narrative approach, links local engagement to issues as diverse as historical research and economic impact. Lastly, the visual incorporation of people walking the footpath sets an inclusive tone, explicitly connecting present-day inhabitants with their ancient counterparts. In the space of four images and a mere 100 words, past and present, contemporary and ancient are both made visible and treated as equally important. This mixing together of elements subsequently set the tone for commentary and contextualisation of the comic in the anthology publication of the *Oswestry Heritage Comics* series:

> People sometimes ask 'What is Wat's Dyke for?'. Borders can be both physical as well as symbolic: the red line at Passport Control, behind which you have to stand before being called forward to the desk, for example. It's not a defensive wall, but it is certainly a border in both legal and psychological terms. Step over that line and there will be consequences. Both Offa's Dyke and Wat's Dyke fall into this kind of category – yes, they were banks and ditches, but they were respected because people understood the consequences in terms of trade and tax - and military

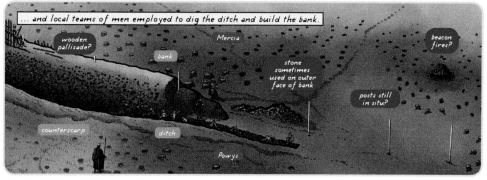

Figure 5: *Building Offa's Dyke*, 2018

Figure 6: Oswestry Heritage Comic: *Oswestry's Other Border* (Swogger 2019a: 8).

retribution. The name 'Wat's Dyke' is a reference to the old English hero Wade (also written Wadda or Wat). Wade was a hero connected with water, so perhaps the fact that Wat's Dyke starts right at the water's edge in Holywell has something to do with this identification. And Wade himself would make a great hero to identify with such a curious construction as the Dyke, snaking its way down the Welsh border. Who but a hero with his magic boat, descended from Wayland the Smith, would make such a thing? I think of Wade – with his semi-divine ancestry, his knack for solving problems and defeating monsters, and his magic travelling machine – as sort of halfway between Thor and Doctor Who. Now there's an idea for a comic! (Swogger 2019a: 8).

Offa's Dyke makes an appearance in two comics. In the first (Figure 7), it features briefly in a discussion about Oswestry's place in the borderlands between England and Wales.

In the second, the Dyke features more centrally in a discussion of the work of the Offa's Dyke Collaboratory (Figure 8).

In this comic, the combination of image and text allowed me to give the research group a human face; the purposes and objectives of the group can be introduced alongside visual and explanatory reminders about its focus; both the local and broader connections of that research can be made explicit, and an inclusive invitation extended to the readership. A comic such as this not only makes the dyke visible, but it makes the process of research and the researchers themselves visible, too. As with those strips in the series which focused on issues of conservation and management at Old Oswestry Hillfort (Swogger 2019a: 3, 12, 19 35, 44, 50) so too could further comics about Offa's Dyke and Wat's Dyke have discussed the monument as a locus for volunteer engagement and community-based stewardship.

The adaptability and flexibility of the medium ensures that even a short-format strip-can have a significant digital and real-world footprint. The ability to promulgate real information about archaeology in a way which is both 'information rich' and yet friendly to modern digital media and vernacular publication is both significant and valuable. It is the reason why, despite still doing plenty of 'traditional' archaeological illustrations, I continue to find new uses for comics within archaeology. This has led me to explore ways in which the broader ability of comics to increase visibility of monuments, research and issues can move beyond public outreach and into the practice of scholarship. Comics used to bring visibility to aspects of scholarship can do all the same things that comics do in public outreach: they add visual context to explanation, introduce and de-complicate subjects, locate specific information within broader frameworks, make connections and links with other research, and even invite participation. Comics can be used to ground and humanise both research and interpretation, something which becomes important if one wishes to present models of past social practice as dynamic, and past landscapes as living places.

Figure 7: *A Borderlands Town* (Swogger 2019a 33).

Figure 8: *Researching Offa's Dyke.* (Swogger 2019a: 42).

Alternative approaches to visualisation can be particularly important in presenting disputed and historically contingent interpretations in archaeology. For example, discussions of the past purpose of Offa's Dyke often consider its implications as a social frontier, as a materialisation of a borderlands between cultures, of a space between Mercia and Powys, between 'Englishness' and 'Welshness", and as a meeting point shaped by the rivalries of power and kinship (e.g. Ray and Bapty 2016: 103; Hill and Worthington 2003: 108; Zalukyj 2011: 187). Such interpretative discussions can lose their impact in text alone. After all, when we talk about marriage or hostage-taking, even wealth or trade, we are talking about events and situations that impact individual lives at the level of emotion: of love, jealousy, ambition, greed and pride. Dispassionate, objective and remote academic text is somewhat unsuited for this kind of discussion. Such interpretations might more successfully frame arguments about how intermarriage or mercantile rivalry might drive Mercian foreign policy, early medieval economics or Anglo-Welsh culture, and thus how they might be reflected in historical and archaeological data if they were rendered in such a way as to highlight their passionate, subjective and intimate nature.

In even a short comic focusing on these things, we can bring to such interpretations historical and cultural grounding, a narrative flow, and a sense of emotional depth, all things which are actually meaningful in the contexts of such discussion (Figure 9).

Such works need be no more than a single page; they need not end up veering away from data towards drama; and it is not necessary to go all *Game of Thrones* in order to make good use of comics in this context. What is needed, however, is recognition that academic text can render significant aspects of our interpretations invisible and thus un-examinable; comics, however, can contribute an important kind of visibility. Such works could act as windows into data and interpretative assumptions and as access points for interdisciplinary collaboration. This might more easily allow economic data, osteological data and survey data to be brought together with anthropology, ethnography and psychology, and make interdisciplinary links more visible by exploiting the way comics utilise narrative and represent temporality. As such, comics have a role to play in an 'intelligently imaginative' borderland between scholarly investigation and creative engagement (cf. Swogger 2019b), 'relaxing our conceptual hold' (Rowland 1976:48) on interpretative and disciplinary structures. Such interpretative presentations can be rendered as easily for academic publication as for popular dissemination, usefully stimulating parallel discussions with different audiences. Affording a different kind of visibility to such interdisciplinary discourse might enable it to reach different kinds of audiences in different ways; the making of comics as a research method in its own right is something which archaeology might benefit from exploring (cf. Sousanis 2015).

Conclusion

The *Oswestry Heritage Comics* provides a model for how it might be possible to increase the visibility of Offa's and Wat's Dyke by using comics. Such an approach could present

Figure 9: *Aehtweligu*, 2018

the dykes within a broad and connected local heritage context, explore contemporary meaning, understand how monuments can hide in plain sight, link with a range of local stakeholders, and connect with research. Such an approach could also operate within a dynamic print and online distribution framework through local news and social media communities. The *Oswestry Heritage Comics* suggest how this reinvention of show and tell could introduce and de-complicate specialist information about Offa's and Wat's Dyke, connecting them with wider historical themes, and signposting ways for the public to become involved in their conservation and management.

Significantly, comics as objects: as comic books, graphic novels, even newspaper strips, are highly portable, meaning the information contained within them can be accessed and re-accessed, read and re-read by audiences without having to make repeat visits to specialist spaces. Unlike interpretation panels, displays or models, they are capable of — literally — staying with their audiences; as 'outreach' they genuinely 'reach out', extending the impact of their informational content beyond the forty-five minutes spent in a visitor centre, or the forty-five seconds spent in front of an on-site interpretation board. Whether aimed at school students or undergraduates, long-distance walkers or museum visitors, academics or council officers, this kind of outreach can be an effective way of taking detailed information on earthwork monuments beyond the museum and the visitor centre.

But the use of comics within archaeology represents a new field of practice and enquiry for the discipline. As an illustrator, I can only take the medium so far. To explore the true potential of comics, to understand its role within public outreach and research, and to evaluate its impact will require more specialist collaboration with and input from other archaeological and heritage professionals. The *Oswestry Heritage Comics* and the examples of comics about Offa's Dyke represent the 'tip of the iceberg': some first steps taken to both explore and shape this medium. Recent and ongoing comics projects continue to suggest new potential in terms of subject matter, approach and audience: *Journeys to Complete the Work* and *Trusting You See This As We Do* (Atalay *et al.* 2017; 2019) address the issue of NAGPRA repatriations and are written and produced in collaboration with Native nations and communities; *Unlocking the Past: Radiocarbon Dating* and *Unlocking the Past: Archaeometallurgy* seek to de-complicate lab-based archaeological science and invite school-age audiences to consider it as a career option (Hunt and Swogger 2016, Hunt *et al.* 2017); *Juigalpa Museum Comics: Exploring Our Indigenous Past* (Geurds and Swogger 2019) actively aligns archaeological investigation of prehispanic Nicaragua with celebration of indigenous culture. *Footprints of the Ancestors* (Napolitano and Swogger 2019) presents soil-science findings from a National Geographic-funded survey and excavation project in the Pacific for a local, community audience.

All these projects are using comics to undertake outreach outside traditional venues for archaeology, science and heritage presentation, bringing information about specific aspects of research into interdisciplinary and non-specialist spaces in order to widen the reach and extend the impact of that information. This kind of outreach can have a transformative impact on not just community-based learning, but community-lead efforts to support archaeology, value science and protect heritage. With the right kind of outreach, 'being interested' can be transformed into a rallying cry for action. There can be a strong connection between information and activism in comics storytelling, giving the medium a unique polemical (and political) role in community-based archaeology and heritage and science communication (Atalay *et al.* in press).

There are, as yet, no long-form graphic works on linear earthworks; there are no studies showing the impact of a series of newspaper comics about Offa's and Wat's Dyke has on community engagement with the monument; no metrics – or, indeed, collections of anecdotes – to help us understand how comics change people's attitudes towards the preservation and study of these monuments. But the work done with comics so far in other contexts strongly suggests that there should be. Even though informational comics are a new medium for archaeological information, there are strong suggestions that they could have an important role to play in outreach. What is needed is for community archaeologists, heritage professionals, researchers and others to engage actively and critically with the medium, testing its potential and discovering both its virtues and its limits.

Comics are not intended to replace any of the existing ways in which we communicate archaeological knowledge, but they do seem to be an effective and meaningful way to talk about aspects of the past which are paradoxically both elusive and highly present. Comics could do more than simply raise awareness about Offa's and Wat's Dyke and other linear earthworks: they could make the complex nature and histories of the monuments themselves, as well as the work of the research communities engaged with them, much more visible.

Bibliography

Atalay, S. 2012. *Community-Based Archaeology*. Berkeley: University of California Press.

Atalay, S., Shannon, J. and Swogger, J. 2017. NAGPRA Comics 1: Journeys To Complete The Work. Amherst: University of Massachusetts Amherst, Boulder: University of Colorado.

Atalay, S., Shannon, J. and Swogger, J. 2019. NAGPRA Comics 2: Trusting You See This As We Do. Amherst: University of Massachusetts Amherst, Boulder: University of Colorado Boulder.

Atalay, S., Bonnano, L., Jacqz, S., Rybka, R., Shannon, J., Speck, C., Swogger, J. and Wolencheck, E. in press. Ethno/Graphic Storytelling: Communicating research and exploring pedagogical Approaches through graphic narratives, drawing and zines. American Anthropologist.

British Broadcasting Corporation (BBC), BBC Radio Shropshire interview, Eric Smith and Clare Ashford Breakfast programme, 8 September 2017, https://www.bbc.co.uk/programmes/p05cphsg

Campbell, E. 2011. *Will Eisner: The Best of Preventive Maintenance Monthly*. New York: Abrams ComicArts.

Geurds, A. and Swogger, J. 2019. *Juigalpa Museum Comics 1: Exploring our Indigenous Past.* Oxford: University of Oxford.

Hosler, J, and Boomer, K.B. 2011. Are Comic Books an Effective Way to Engage Nonmajors in Learning and Appreciating Science? *CBE Life Sciences Education* 10(3): 309-17.

Hill, D. and Worthington, M. 2003. *Offa's Dyke: History and Guide.* Stroud: Tempus.

Hunt, A. and Swogger, J. 2016. *Unlocking the Past 1: Radiocarbon Dating.* Athens: University of Georgia, Centre for Applied Isotope Studies.

Hunt, A., Speakman, J. and Swogger, J. 2017. *Unlocking the Past 2: Archaeometallurgy.* Athens: University of Georgia, Centre for Applied Isotope Studies.

McCloud, S. 1993. Understanding Comics. Northampton: Kitchen Sink Press.

McCloud, S. 2006. *Making Comics.* New York: Harper.

McNicol, S. 2017. The potential of educational comics as a health information medium. *Health Information and Libraries Journal* 34(1): 20-31.

Napolitano, M. and Swogger, J. 2019. Footprints of the Ancestors. University of Oregon: National Geographic.

Ray, K. and Bapty, I. 2016. *Offa's Dyke. Landscape and Hegemony in Eighth-Century Britain,* Oxford: Oxbow.

Rowland, K. 1976. *Visual Education and Beyond.* London: Ginn and Company.

Shanks, M. 1997. Photography and archaeology, in B. Molyneaux (ed.) *The Cultural Life of Images*: London: Routledge: 73-107.

Sousanis, N. 2015. *Unflattening.* Boston: Harvard University Press.

Swogger, J. 2000. Image and interpretation: the tyranny of representation? in I. Hodder (ed.) *Towards Reflexive Method in Archaeology: The Example at Çatalhöyük. British Institute of Archaeology at Ankara* Monograph No. 28. Cambridge: McDonald Institute for Archaeological Research: 143-152.

Swogger, J. 2019a. *The Oswestry Heritage Comics.* Oswestry: Qube/Oswestry Community Action.

Swogger, J. 2019b. Creativity, community and the past: engaging public audiences through heritage comics, in G. Nash (ed.), in press.

Swogger, J. 2019c. Homefront Heroines. Oswestry: Qube/Oswestry Community Action, Oswestry Advertizer.

Zalukyj, S. 2011. *Mercia.* Hereford: Logaston Press.

John G. Swogger, Archaeologist and Artist
    Email: jgswogger@gmail.com